Manoeuvres in Moscow
Karpov-Kasparov II

RAYMOND KEENE
DAVID GOODMAN

B.T.Batsford Ltd, *London*

First published 1985
Reprinted 1985
© Raymond Keene and David Goodman 1985

ISBN 0 7134 5379 6(limp)

Photoset by Andek Printing, London
and printed in Great Britain by
Billings Ltd, Worcester
for the publishers
B.T.Batsford Ltd, 4 Fitzhardinge Street,
London W1H OAH

to Peter Pitt and Ian McNicoll

A BATSFORD CHESS BOOK

Adviser: R.D.Keene
Technical Editor: P.A.Lamford

Contents

Acknowledgements

Our thanks to Annette Keene for typing the book; Andek for their usual efficient typesetting; Bob Wade for midnight references; Paul Lamford for editing and proofreading the text; Ed Harriman for many helpful suggestions; Morris Needleman, President of the Australian Chess Federation, for providing the photo of Karpov and Kasparov; Fabio Biagi for the photos of the authors; David Anderton for notes on Campomanes' press conference in London; Radames Kulenović for providing material from the exchange of open letters between Gligorić and Kasparov; Jon Tisdall of Reuters, Edie Lederer of AP (London), AP Moscow Bureau chief Roxinne Ervasti for use of telex facilities, and everyone at the Moscow Bureau of AP for their friendly co-operation; Associated Press, the *Times*, the *Guardian*, the *Spectator*, the *Financial Times*, Novosti, CNN and *Chess Life* for permission to quote material; finally, Dr Nikolai Krogius, Chairman of the USSR Chess Federation, for his kind invitation to Moscow.

Raymond Keene, David Goodman
London, November 1985

"As you settle down behind your pawns, power passes to me.
You may play like Fischer, Capablanca, Tal combined, I don't mind, please feel free.
They all thought they were the big fromage, but they don't have my clout.
I control the match, I start it, I can call it off, Kasparov found that out."

Tim Rice, *The Arbiter's Song*, from his musical *CHESS*

ONE

The Press Conference

Moscow (February)

On 10 September 1984 the Karpov-Kasparov World Chess Championship commenced in Moscow.* Karpov, then 33, is slightly built, a model Soviet citizen, chairman of the Soviet Peace Fund, and has received the Order of Lenin. Kasparov is twelve years younger, half Armenian, half Jewish, outspoken, brash and unpredictable on and off the board. Their clash had been billed by many (including ourselves) as potentially the most fascinating chess contest since Fischer against Spassky in 1972. But after a five-month marathon the Championship was terminated by Florencio Campomanes, the Filipino President of the World Chess Federation (FIDE) and a keen student of President Marcos' speeches. The score was, at that stage, five wins to Karpov, three to Kasparov, with 40 draws. The world title should have gone to the player who first achieved six wins. Apart from this restriction the match was unlimited. After 27 games the score was 5-0 in Karpov's favour, but he failed to score a single win after 24 November, while Kasparov won three times, including crushing victories in what turned out to be the last two games of the match, 47 and 48.

Over 8 and 9 February, Kasparov won his third game (his second in succession). Campomanes flew suddenly from Dubai to Moscow and then came a week of "time-outs" with no play. Tension and speculation mounted amongst the world's chess fraternity and the media flocked back to Moscow.

On Friday 15 February the crunch came – a press conference called by Campomanes at noon Moscow time in the Hotel Sport. The match had earlier been shifted to this concrete suburban fortress after the managers of the prestigious Hall of Columns (the original venue) had demanded their site back. Around 300 journalists were present. Campomanes told them that he had decided to stop the match. There follows the full text of that amazing confrontation between the FIDE President, the players and the world's press. The transcript comes from tapes supplied by Cable News Network.

MODERATOR: The floor is given to our esteemed President, President of FIDE, Mr Campomanes.

* *See* The Moscow Challenge, *the book on the first Karpov-Kasparov match, by R.D.Keene (B.T.Batsford, 1985)*

1

CAMPOMANES: Good afternoon, ladies and gentlemen of the press and broadcast media. First of all, I apologise for the delay. This reminds me of the time I had been elected President in Lucerne in 1982. The day after, I was supposed to name the Secretary General and as is normal in these matters there were many options. When I got to my seat in the conference hall to make my announcement, up until I was before the microphone I did not know whom I was going to choose – Mr Clues of Wales, Mr Keene of England, Mr Kažić of Yugoslavia or Professor Lim Kok Ann of Singapore. No one believed me when I said I didn't know what to do – whom to choose – up until that final moment, and I suppose many of you will be good doubting Thomases when I also tell you to this very moment, I do not know. This match, this current world chess championship match, has been an unusual competition which created unusual problems demanding special solutions. Whereas in accordance with FIDE statutes the President is empowered to take decisions in between congresses and whereas under the match regulations the President is personally and officially responsible for the entire match, and further is empowered to take the final decision on all questions affecting the match as a whole, I therefore declare that the match is ended without decision. A new match shall be played from scratch – zero-zero – starting 1 September 1985 (*much talk in the audience*), starting September 1985.

QUESTIONER: Whose consent?

CAMPOMANES: The two players' consent. The next FIDE Congress in August shall determine further necessary match provisions – the winner of that match will be the Champion for the period 1985-86. Thank you.

(*Kasparov began talking with his camp and once or twice laughed quietly*)

QUESTIONER: What are the reasons for the early ending of the match?

CAMPOMANES: I think there was a glimpse in the statement. This has been a match that beat the record of all other matches – the greatest number of games, the greatest number of draws, more than five months' duration. It has exhausted the physical, if not the psychological, resources not only of the participants but all those connected with the match, however distant that connection might be.

I for one have not been fully able to perform my functions and fulfil my other duties as President of FIDE 'cause this has hovered over all my activities.

QUESTIONER: Is Mr Karpov unable to continue the match?

CAMPOMANES (smiling): I wish you had the possibility of tracking me down during the last hour because then you would have found a ready answer to that question.

(*8-second pause*)

QUESTIONER: Well, sir, if you don't answer the question . . .

CAMPOMANES: Just a minute, sir, I have not finished. Mr Karpov is well and appealed to me to continue with the match till the very end on

2

Monday. I left him no longer than 25 minutes ago and I just told one of my colleagues here behind me that I make this decision despite him. As all of you know very well, or have suspected, or have accused, that I am a very good friend of Mr Karpov – you are right – but that has nothing to do with what I feel is best for chess in the world. I denied his request. I don't need witnesses for this, but I have witnesses – let that be clear. Mr Karpov was ready 25 minutes ago and told me to please not play today 'cause Mr Kasparov and he are psychologically unprepared for today 'cause of all this brouhaha. He asked to start playing Monday, to the better or bitter end and that is what I meant when I told you on the podium that that was not what I was going to do.

QUESTIONER: What was the Challenger's response?

CAMPOMANES: I have conferred with the Challenger – I treat them as equal participants in this match – I am certain he is not happy about the decision either. But it is the challenge in accordance with the regulations for the President to take a decision as best he knows – to the dismay, maybe, of many of those involved, but decision he must take. He cannot be expected to please everybody or anybody but he must take a decision. And now I understand without abrogation to myself the wisdom of Solomon – how he felt when he held that baby in his hands. Thank you.

Yes, Mr Doder, how are you this morning? I was trying to get hold of you 'cause I wanted to keep my word but I've been confined this morning as you might well understand.

QUESTIONER: I appreciate. In your own words, Mr Campomanes, both the Champion and the Challenger want to play. Can you tell us by what right are you taking the decision? Explain a bit more. What are the special circumstances?

CAMPOMANES: Thank you, Mr Doder, I think I so much, in so many words, replied to you yesterday and I repeated it on the podium. The right is clear. The reasons – first we are thinking of the two best players of the world. We are thinking of chess as a sport in the eyes of the world. We are thinking of the well-being of all those connected with the match in Moscow and elsewhere, and other considerations bordering on this theme. I quote Mr Mydans who was trying to get hold of me yesterday. I understand but I was not around. In your editorial, in your report in *The New York Times*, 29 January, you yourself said that this was becoming not a test of chess skill, but a matter of physical endurance. I recall when the score was 5-0 and so many games had been played everybody was saying when will this end and then more draws happened and then Mr Kasparov won a game and then more draws – everybody was knocking at the door saying let's end this match and now that we end the match you ask me why. I think the question answers itself.

QUESTIONER: I have two questions. Thank you for calling the position of the two players regarding the decision. Could you tell us please how the Soviet Federation reacted to this proposal? And how can the ending

3

of the game, when both players want to play, benefit the sport?

CAMPOMANES: I'll only answer one of your questions – the other has been answered. The USSR Chess Federation agrees with my decision.

QUESTIONER (Richard Owen, Moscow Correspondent of The Times*):* Mr Campomanes, I just wonder how you respond to suggestions from qualified commentators such as Raymond Keene that if Mr Karpov is unable to stand the pressure after six months he should have resigned his title given that chess is not only a matter of skill and moves but also of psychological pressure and a matter of endurance over a period of time – and also given that Mr Kasparov doesn't look like a man who is psychologically or physically shattered? *(laughter from audience)*

CAMPOMANES: First of all, you quote Mr Keene. What is the date of that thinking?

QUESTIONER: He made this remark in my newspaper, *The Times*, two days ago.

CAMPOMANES: I was with Mr Keene four and a half days ago in Dubai and we had thrown this back and forward over good red wine and then I was on the phone again with him two nights ago – he's back in England. And Mr Keene is a Grandmaster of England, your second, and he is entitled to this opinion and that's what makes FIDE such a jolly family – we agree to disagree.

*QUESTIONER (*Tass*):* What is the most efficient regulation system of the match?

CAMPOMANES: That's a good question *(laughter from audience)*. If I may remind your memory, your good servant was the organiser for the Philippine Chess Federation of the 1978 World Championship match. At the time we thought it was such a long match and I can assure you I can understand here how the organising committee here feels – because I thought at the end of 93 days I was ready to collapse and now this is more than 150 days. But the regulations served that championship, the regulations served the championship in Merano, but as I keep telling my close associates the fact that it has lasted this long is not the fault of the regulations. The regulations may be well and good, but happily – I say happily – the excellence of the players has reached such a level that they have discovered the secret of how to draw, to minimise to the barest of minimums the risk of losing. It is the excellence of present-day chess. If there is anyone one can fault it is the particular excellence that has contributed to the length of the match – forty draws, unheard of in previous matches. So the regulations being the product of human considerations cannot expect to fulfil all situations. That is why there is present in these regulations that somebody has to be personally and officially responsible to look at the events from all standpoints, and hope to goodness he makes the right decision.

*QUESTIONER (*Sovietsky Sport*):* How does he explain the situation that has arisen during the match, for clarification – but you have made an assessment of the match?

4

CAMPOMANES (after consulting a Soviet official for further clarification):
Ah yes! Thank you very much, it is a good question. We have reached a
junction where we have technically two times the size of the match of the
previous regulation – 24 games. This is 48 games, it is a good junction to
pause and give thought. That is why I saw the need to take action –
because from here on what do you use – 72 games? Anything can happen
when the match shall have lasted that long. I don't envy the press people
themselves. I remember the first days and all the bustle of activity in the
press centre. Before I went to Dubai I visited the press centre. It didn't
look like the local morgue (*he laughs*) but there were very much less
people in the press centre. You do get tired yourselves.

QUESTIONER: You said that the players have discovered the secret of
how to draw, but you arrived here just when Mr Kasparov seemed to
have discovered the secret of how to win. Doesn't this give the
impression that you came at the last moment to save Mr Karpov?

CAMPOMANES: Saving him from himself? No. I have been giving
thought to this much earlier. From the point of the 32nd game I began
thinking of this. I recall Baguio was 32 games and I needed more input
and I had been called away on trips requiring my attention. All of this
began to jell when we were talking very much about this in Athens and I
had received all kinds of telephone calls from chess leaders all round the
world. 24 times two is 48. This is an excellent junction to take stock
independent of what you call the trend of the match – because like all
trends doing the stock market, which goes up and down, you never know
when it will take a nose-dive.

QUESTIONER: I just want to know how you feel personally about the
decision given that both players say they want to continue the match?

CAMPOMANES: Yes, lady. My decision was taken equally for both
players. You can't expect to please everybody, or even anybody. Up till that
moment I didn't know. I have to live with myself and I sleep very well.

*QUESTIONER (*Sovietsky Sport*):* Another question about the
regulations. So far twenty-nine matches have been played, the biggest
one of 34 games. The system seemed to be appropriate – all the chess
public approved of that system. Why was that system changed? And
what system do you consider the most optimal?

CAMPOMANES: I believe I alluded to that indirectly earlier. Any
regulation is used – it is the proof of the pudding that counts. When it is
applied, given the circumstances, some regulations function well and
others falter or fail, and moreover this is the prerogative eventually of the
conference of FIDE to which I must defer. They formulate the regulations,
starting with the committees and end with a unanimous vote or a show
of hands. Regulations are only regulations. People make them; circumstances affect them.

QUESTIONER: I would like to ask just one question – which you
alluded to earlier. There have been more specific reports on some of the
wire services recently that Mr Karpov was on the verge of a psychological

breakdown, (*at this point Campomanes smiled and rose*) that he was exhausted and so forth. Would you address yourself to those – that he was in a hospital bed?

CAMPOMANES (standing and having taken the microphone): You asked the question at the very right time – Mr Karpov is there behind you, now just arrived.

(From the back of the hall Karpov said in Russian "I want to make a statement". As he walked to the stage there was loud applause from the audience. Gligorić gave up his seat and Karpov shook hands with a smiling Campomanes and with the Foreign Ministry man at the press conference. Karpov sat down next to Campomanes.)

KARPOV: I must tell you, as we Russians say, the rumours about my death were a bit exaggerated.

CAMPOMANES: Anatoly, I just told him about that.

KARPOV: And I consider that we can and we ought to continue the match – and the proposal to end it and start from scratch, I do not agree with it (*applause from audience*). I consider that on Monday February 18 we should start, or rather resume and continue, our match. I think Kasparov will second my proposal and there should be no problem at all (*applause*).

CAMPOMANES (smiling): Gentlemen, now you know what I told you earlier was true. I have a verification right here in the friend – in the person – of the World Champion. I have mentioned this to you and now Mr Kasparov will know that I now told you the truth.

KARPOV: I think we should invite Kasparov here (*with a hand gesture*).

FOREIGN MINISTRY SPOKESMAN: But the decision is taken.

CAMPOMANES: Gary, you want to come and say your piece?

(Kasparov tried to speak from the audience, but could not be heard without a microphone and started towards the podium. As Kasparov walked down the stairs, Campomanes could clearly be heard on the tape to say:)

CAMPOMANES: I told them exactly what you told me to tell them.*

KARPOV: We . . . we, but I don't accept this.

(Kasparov arrived at the podium to much applause as Campomanes talked with Sevastianov)

KASPAROV: I want to ask Mr President one question – what all that show is for? Mr President, I shall explain what I mean. You said you have come here 25 minutes after your talk with the Champion and he was against breaking the match. You knew my point of view too – that I was also objecting to ending or suspending the match with technical time-outs. Nevertheless, you came here and declared your point of view that, despite all those objections, the game is ended. What do we need it for? Twenty-five minutes ago you were speaking with Karpov and now

---

* *Campomanes later explained that he had added the words "that you wanted to continue". Unfortunately, this remark was not picked up by the CNN tapes.*

suddenly such a divergence. Will you tell us, or at least me?

CAMPOMANES: I personally believe that what I was doing was in the best interests. But the players are only one part of this situation. Now, however . . . (*after some hesitation*) however, I am in a very happy position right now. I am in a position that I couldn't have wished for better. If the two players are willing to play to the very end (*laughter from audience*) I will consider in a conversation with the two of them alone because I have long demanded this situation to happen and I have not been able to get it, because Mr Karpov is not available, Mr Kasparov is not available, and I tried to get them. As a matter of fact, as late as last night I tried to get them together, but Mr Kasparov is sleeping – Mr Karpov has been often times in accordance with the meeting schedule. Now we have it. Now I want to talk with both of you (*applause*). Let's have ten minutes inside.

(Karpov and Campomanes stood up. Campomanes held out both his arms in a gesture to the audience. Simultaneously, Kasparov held out his hand, palm forward, to make a stop sign.)

KASPAROV: Give me the floor. I want to make known my declaration. The President's profession is to speak. My trade is to play chess. That is why I am not going to compete with him on the podium – first. (*speaking very quickly and angrily*) Second, I want to say what I think. I don't intend to demand a continuation because I'm convinced I shall win very easily because the Champion feels unwell. He's here, he can proceed, we can see it. But for the first time in five months I have certain chances, let's say about 25% or 30%, and now they are trying to deprive me of those chances by the numerous delays – and let those who delayed the match be responsible. The match should continue – I have been speaking about it two weeks ago – without time-outs, without intervals, but it is being prolonged. With each delay his chances are growing while mine are diminishing (*applause*).

FOREIGN MINISTRY SPOKESMAN: The Press Conference is over. (*much laughter from audience, and after a few seconds' thought he said:*) If the President considers it appropriate to continue . . .

CAMPOMANES: If Mr Kasparov refuses to have a huddle with me I cannot change the decision. With me and Mr Karpov – as clear as that. The decision stands if the two do not sit down and talk about it and shake on it.

(Karpov walked back)

KARPOV: I can make my own statement.

CAMPOMANES (to Karpov): You play today?

KARPOV: No.

CAMPOMANES: Monday?

KARPOV: Monday.

FOREIGN MINISTRY SPOKESMAN: It's better to have a rest.

KARPOV: I think we can make a sort of break now for everybody to calm down (*applause*). And after the interval announce the final

decision.
CAMPOMANES: A break of ten minutes.

(Final statement, after a one-hour interval:)
CAMPOMANES: This is more than just Solomonic dilemma, it is a Gordian knot put on top of it. The World Champion accepts the decision of the President and the Challenger abides by the decision of the President. In the course of the meeting I have appreciated the thinking of the World Champion who feels very strongly that he deserves, or has a right to, a return match after the new match. I have appreciated likewise the strong wish of the Challenger that the provisions for the next match be ascertained fully since he felt that leaving it hanging in Congress or for the decision of the FIDE Congress in September, in August, is not the most suitable arrangement for him. The Congress of FIDE shall take place in Graz, Vienna, in Graz, Austria, and will end before the match begins. It may be the same day the match begins. I have committed myself to the two players to make this known to Congress and I add on my own, not only to Congress, but to the leadership of the 122 Federations of FIDE, that in accepting on the part of the World Champion and abiding on the part of the Challenger to this decision they have made fully known their thinking on these matters. I thank you.

TWO

The Official Version

Lucerne (March)

On 11 March 1985 the FIDE President's circular letter number 4 went out to the 120-plus member nations of the World Chess Federation. The bulk of it was devoted to the official explanation and documents pertaining to the ending of the match.

" . . .

President's Circular Letter No. 4, 1984/85.
11 March 1985.

World Championship Match Terminated

On 15 February a media conference was held in the Sports Hotel, Moscow, the venue to which the World Championship Match had been moved in early February. FIDE President stated that the current match had been an unusual competition that created unusual problems demanding special solutions. The President of FIDE, he said, is empowered to act on behalf of FIDE between congresses, and is personally and officially responsible for the entire match, including its preparation and conclusion. According to Regulation D.I.06, Art. 6.11, the President "is empowered to take the final decision in all questions affecting the match as a whole." The President then made the following declaration:

1. The Match is ended without decision.
2. A new match shall be played from scratch, from 0-0 score, starting September 2nd, 1985.
3. FIDE Congress in Graz, August, will determine further necessary regulations.
4. The winner of that match will be World Champion for 1985/86.

After the 48 games and 160 days, yielding 40 draws and only 8 decisions, the President received a letter from the USSR Chess Federation which requested that the match be suspended. The score was 5 wins for Karpov and 3 wins for Kasparov.

The President had been away from Moscow on a FIDE mission to the Middle East. He returned on February 11 to find that Kasparov had called a time-out. It had been evident that the prolonged match had drained the physical and psychological resources of all involved in the match, not only of the players. At the same time the level of excellence of the games no longer attained earlier heights. In consultation with the Chief Arbiter and the Chairman of the Appeals Committee, the President undertook discussions with the players and the organizers. To gain time for further consultations the President cancelled the game scheduled for 13 February. On 15 February the President called the media conference.

It must be appreciated that FIDE was bound to accept the official statement of the USSR Chess Federation that the health of the players would be endangered if the match be allowed to continue. FIDE is primarily responsible to the national federation representing the players, and the personal wishes of the players come next. Since the USSR Chess Federation represented both the World Champion and the Challenger, FIDE had no alternative but to consider this and other alternatives. Although the USSR Chess Federation had requested a suspension only, the President felt that this would be the same as a long "time-out" whereas the regulations provide for only a limited number of "time-outs". If the match could not be allowed to continue, then the right thing to do was to completely end it. With this decision, a majority of the members of the Executive Council concurred.

Arriving late to the media conference, the World Champion declared, on being invited by the President to the platform, that he was ready to continue the match. This surprised the Challenger who had earlier remained silent, seated in an upper row in the conference room, and who then arose and stated that he, too, wished the match to continue. Thereupon, the President recessed the media conference so as to consult with the players together. Though he had tried hard in the past three days to achieve this, the President had succeeded only in meeting them individually.

After an hour, the President informed the press and broadcast media that the World Champion accepted the President's decision, and the Challenger abided by it. In accepting the decision, Mr. Karpov stated that he wished it known that he expressed his request that the Graz Congress should affirm his right to a return match, should he lose the September match. Mr. Kasparov, on his part, wished it to be known that he had asked for a definite decision on the conditions of the match well before the match is played.

And the decision stood.   . . . "

A number of annexes were attached to this circular letter. The documents relevant to the termination of the World Championship match are now given in their original (frequently misspelled!) form. It is interesting that FIDE itself should have presented the *decision* to terminate and the *request* to terminate in this order.

1. Press statement, Moscow, 15.02.85

" . . .

The current World Chess Championship Match has been an unusual competition which created unusual problems demanding special solutions.

Whereas, in accordance with FIDE Statutes, the President is empowered to take decisions between congresses and, whereas, under the Match Regulations the President is personally and officially responsible for the entire match /1.21/ and, further, is empowered to take the final decision on all questions affecting the match as a whole /6.11/,

I declare that:

> a/ The Match is ended without decision.

> b/ A new Match shall be played from scratch, /0-0/, starting on September 1st 1985. The next FIDE congress in August shall determine further necessary Match provisions.
> The winner of that Match shall be the World Champion for the period 1985-1986.

F.Campomanes
FIDE President . . . "

2. USSR Chess Federation's request for suspension of match, 13.02.85

" . . .

To: FIDE President
Mr. Campomanes

Taking into consideration the unpresedented duration of the World Chess Match between A.Karpov and G.Kasparov, which now has exceeded 5 months with 48 games played / e.g. two full time matches as per the old regulations /, the Soviet Chess Federation – expressing worry about health status of the players – requests 3-month suspension of the match.

As it is known, the terms of the unlimited match Fischer vs. Karpov /1976/ contained provision for the break after 4 months of continious game. This provision had been included on the basis of opinion by medical experts. But the duration of the match Karpov vs. Kasparov – as it was mentioned above – is longer and the match is still underway.

May we note also, that proposal to suspend the match does not contradict both FIDE Regulations and the reglament of the match; [therefore] we believe, that this proposal will be accepted with satisfaction by the world chess community.

Your positive decision will contribute into futher development of chess creativity.

Respectfully Yours,
Chairman,
USSR Chess Federation;
twice Hero of the Soviet Union
Pilot-Cosmonaut
V.I.Sevestyanov . . . "

3. Karpov's telexed open letter requesting the match be resumed, 19.02.85

" . . .

DEAR MR. PRESIDENT,

IN CONTINUATION OF OUR DISCUSSIONS DURING YOUR RECENT VISIT TO MOSCOW I WOULD LIKE ONCE AGAIN TO SAY THAT I HIGHLY APPRECIATE YOUR CONCERN ABOUT THE HEALTH AND NERVES OF THE PLAYERS AND ALL THOSE CONNECTED WITH UNPRECEDENTEDLY PROLONGED MATCH. I UNDERSTAND HUMAN MOTIVES THAT INFLUENCED YOUR DECISION TO END THE MATCH.

YOU, NO DOUBT, ACTED IN THE INTERESTS OF CHESS, BUT I AM DEEPLY CONVINCED THAT THE PRESENT SITUATION HAS CAUSED DAMAGE TO CHESS TO SAY NOTHING OF BLASTING MY SPORTS AND PUBLIC REPUTATION WHICH IN THE COURSE OF MANY YEARS HAS BEEN CONSIDERED UNIMPEACHABLE. UNFORTUNATELY, SOME PUBLIC STATEMENTS OF THE CHALLENGER CONDUCE TO THAT.

IN ITS APPROACH TO YOU THE USSR CHESS FEDERATION HAS NOT PROPOSED TO END THE MATCH BUT ONLY TO MAKE A BRAKE WHICH COULD HAVE ENABLED ALL THE PEOPLE CONCERNED TO HAVE A REST.

AS YOU KNOW ON FEBRUARY 15 1985 BOTH THE PLAYERS HAVE EXPRESSED THEIR STRONG WISH AND ABILITY TO CONTINUE PLAYING TILL THE FINAL RESULT PROVIDED FOR IN THE REGULATIONS APPROVED BY THE FIDE CONGRESS. FOR ME, PERSONALLY, THIS POSSIBILITY IS NECESSARY IN ORDER TO ONCE AGAIN PROVE MY ADHERENCE TO THE PRINCIPLES OF SPORTS COMPETITION OVER THE CHESSBOARD. THE CHALLENGER HAS HIS OWN ARGUMENTS: HE IS COMPLAINING OF BEING DELIBERATELY DEPRIVED OF HIS RIGHT TO COMPETE FOR THE HIGHEST TITLE.

I AM SURE THAT MILLIONS OF CHESS ENTHUSIASTS ARE NOT SATISFIED BY THE FACT THAT THE SPORTS COMPETITION HAS REMAINED UNFINISHED. CONSEQUENTLY, RESUMPTION OF THE MATCH WILL BE FOR GENERAL BENEFIT.

I HOPE THAT THE USSR CHESS FEDERATION IN THESE CIRCUMSTANCES WILL NOT OPPOSE TO THE WISH OF ITS OWN STRONGEST CHESSPLAYERS. IT IS CERTAINLY NOT IN THE INTERESTS OF THE FEDERATION FOR THE ATMOSPHERE TO BE HEATED.

IT HAS NOT BEEN EASY FOR YOU TO TAKE YOUR DECISION ON FEBRUARY 15, 1985, AND NATURALLY IT IS NOT EASY FOR YOU NOW TO REVIEW IT. BUT DURING THE CANDIDATES' COMPETITIONS IN 1983 YOU ALREADY PROVED YOUR WISDOM AND ABILITY TO PLACE THE INTERESTS OF CHESS AND CHESSPLAYERS ABOVE ALL.

12

THAT HAS ONLY SERVED TO CONSOLIDATION OF YOUR PRESTIGE AND AUTHORITY.

KEEPING THIS IN MIND I APPEAL TO YOU TO GIVE YOUR CONSENT TO RESUMPTION OF THE PLAY IN THE MATCH AS SOON AS IT IS ONLY POSSIBLE.

SINCERELY YOURS,

ANATOLY KARPOV
WORLD CHAMPION . . . "

4. The President's telex to Moscow, 21.02.85

" . . .

ATTENTION USSR CHESS FEDERATION.

CONCERNING MR. KARPOV'S OPEN LETTER DATED 19 FEBRUARY, PRESIDENT WISHES TO KNOW YOUR VIEWS ON HIS REQUEST TO HAVE MATCH RESUMED, THAT IS, ARE YOU READY TO REORGANIZE MATCH, IF HYPOTHETICALLY PRESIDENT DECIDES AFFIRMATIVELY ON MR. KARPOV'S REQUEST.

FURTHER, PRESIDENT WOULD LIKE TO SOLICIT THROUGH YOU, SINCE PRESIDENT HAS NOW NO WAY TO CONTACT MR. KASPAROV, HIS VIEWS ON POSSIBLE RESUMPTION OF MATCH.

REGARDS
DR. LIM KOK ANN
GENERAL SECRETARY . . . "

5. USSR Chess Federation's offers

" . . .
F.CAMPOMANES
FIDE PRESIDENT

WE REQUEST TO GRANT THE RIGHT FOR THE ORGANISATION OF THE MATCH FOR THE WORLD CHAMPION TITLE BETWEEN ANATOLY KARPOV AND GARRY KASPAROV ACCORDING TO THE REGULATIONS TO BE APPROVED BY 1985 FIDE CONGRESS, TO THE USSR CHESS FEDERATION. START OF THE MATCH FIRST WEEK OF SEPTEMBER 1985

WITH BEST REGARDS
V.SEVASTYANOV
USSR CHESS FEDERATION . . . "

" . . .
LIM KOK ANN
FIDE GENERAL SECRETARY

PLEASE CONVEY TO THE FIDE PRESIDENT F.CAMPOMANES THAT IN CASE HE TAKES A DECISION TO RESUME THE MATCH KARPOV KASPAROV THE USSR CHESS FEDERATION AND THE ORGANIZING COMMITTEE FOR THE MATCH ARE READY TO CONTINUE THEIR ACTIVITIES.

13

AS FAR AS COOORDINATION OF OPINIONSEEE OPINIONS OF THE WORLS CHAMPION AND THE CHALLENGER IS THE PREROGATIVE OF THE PRESIDENT WE ASK HIM TO CONTACT THEN PERSONALLY. KASPAROV WILL STAY IN MOSCOW TILL FEBRUARY 27th.

REGARDS
USSR CHESS FEDERATION . . . ”

6. Telexed information from Kasparov

“ . . .

ATT. MR. AVANCENO

MOST URGENT, FOR MR. CAMPOMANES, PHILCHESS, THANK YOU.

MESSAGE FROM GLIGORIC:

GLIGORIC HAS CONTACTED MAMEDOV, CHIEF KASPAROV DELEGATION, IN MOSCOW.

MAMEDOV IN KASPAROV’S NAME SAID KASPAROV DOES NOT WANT TO CONTINUE THE MATCH.

KASPAROV ACCEPTS DECISION OF FIDE PRESIDENT TO CONSIDER MATCH ENDED.

KASPAROV IS READY TO PLAY NEW MATCH IN SEPTEMBER.

MESSAGE ENDS.

RGDS. LIMKOKANN, FIDE GENSEC. /RAK . . . ”

7. President’s Manila press statement

“ . . .

I have within the last nine days been receiving requests to alter the February 15th decision to end the match without decision, and to start a new match on Sept. 2, 1985. Foremost, and most direct and most persistent has been from Mr. Anatoly Karpov. You are familiar with the reasons for that decision? Let us review them . . .

What reasons could there be for a change of that decision? Why should we resume the match from where we left off?

On Feb. 19, Karpov had an open letter for me which he had distributed to media in Moscow. (I actually read it in full on the 21st in Athens). This circumstance alone is unprecedented, and deserved total attention. Note the emotional tone. He wishes to redeem his blasted sports and public reputation.

Mr. Kasparov never formally entered a protest. His protestations during the media conference on Feb. 15th must have been tentative and ill considered outbursts, reacting to Mr. Karpov’s earlier call for a continuation of the match.

14

Have the conditions changed today to warrant a reversal? They will still play an unlimited match till one player wins six. What's the prospect, 1, 5, a dozen or even thirty games. If Karpov wins, fine, but if Karpov loses, can the revanche match be played September?

Assuming it is resumed, they'll play, say by March first. Two weeks interval. Mr. Karpov shall have rested, it can be alleged.

Will the former excellence of play be revived. This is moot.

The only certain change is that media will cover it once more in grand style. For a while anyway, until they get bored with prospective draws.

Alternatives and some possible EFFECTS:

A. If I become convinced of the wisdom of the proponents of resumption, or succumb to the fleeting but fierce pressures of "The show must go on " groups, the galeria can once again shout "Ole" as they see blood on sand.

The organizing committee will dutifully renew preparations and in quick time place Sports Hotel or Trade Union hall in full match gear . . . telexes, extra phones for media . . . and track down the other principals of the match (Oh, yes, there are people other than the players involved) from Yugoslavia, Germany, Spain and the Philippines (assuming they've made no other commitments) and bring them back to Moscow. These are not insurmountable tasks.

Mr. Karpov will have a chance to redeem, to paraphrase him, his blasted sports and public reputation.

And Mr. Kasparov will have his opportunity to gamble with his 25 or 30% chance to win the match.

And everyone will be convinced of the truth that Mr. Karpov truly wanted on Feb. 15 to continue playing to the end; and that it was he who first declared publicly that the match should continue, not Mr. Kasparov, on that memorable day, Feb. 15.

The gallery shall have been served and the match games and their sidelights shall be grist for media's mill.

B. In FIDE's name I should stand resolute on the decision of Feb. 15, as I am buffeted by fierce opinion favoring match resumption, I risk unpopularity or outright condemnation. To this I pay little heed. It's a hazard of office. Have I not spoused seemingly unpopular decisions before!

I risk unafraid because FIDE must see beyond the forest, and render decisions that long endure. But most of all I risk the loss of a long-standing friendship with Mr. Karpov . . .

15

Therefore I opted on Feb. 15, to paraphrase Mr. Golombek of the London Times, for the only practical way of solving the problem with which I was faced.

Today I choose to reinforce that option: ending the match without decision, and starting a new match from scratch (0-0) on Sept. 2, 1985. From the innermost in heart and mind, I firmly believe it was right then, it is right today, and only time will give its final verdict.

Am sorry, Tolya.

Gens Una Sumus.

Florencio Campomanes
FIDE President . . . "

8. Extract from report of Chief Arbiter, S.Gligorić

" . . .
Annex B is Mr. Kinzel's presentation of that what happened during the most significant period between February 1 and 15. Instead of writing it myself, I took the liberty of translating personally the major part of that text from German into English for FIDE members' information, for I share Mr. Kinzel's opinion about those facts.

To that Annex B I could only add the following remark: had the champion accepted the challenger's counter-proposal on February 4 (while the FIDE President was in Dubai), we would have the situation which we have today, but with all parties concerned in happy agreement. It could have happened, and I am very sorry that it did not. Perhaps, I hoped for too much, having in mind normal over-sensitivity of two great contestants after their almost superhuman efforts in five long months resulting also in increased frequency of technical mistakes in certain games.

With additional requirements of both participants there was no agreement in sight, and the end of the match, "imposed" by the FIDE President, was followed by words of protest, unnecessary disagreements, and sharp criticisms here and there in the world press. If there was any profit from that, it could be the increased publicity around chess, that the conflict of opinions provoked . .

The FIDE President left Moscow on February 2 and arrived back on February 11. After 4 days of consultations with all parties concerned, using his legal power, he declared on the press conference of February 15, 1985, that the "match is ended without decision". It meant that after 48 games (which is double the normal match with limited number of games) no contest succeeded in obtaining the required 6 wins. I think that wrong wordings were used about that in the meantime. The match neither was

16

"interrupted" (then, it would continue after a rest period), nor "annuled", since it was played being the longest match ever, only the question of the future title holder has remained open. Therefore, the decision of Mr. Campomanes is completed by "the new match (on different system, approved by the next FIDE Congress) will be played in September-October 1985".

Belgrade, February 26-28, 1985

(Svetozar Gligorić)
Chief Arbiter of the
match Karpov-Kasparov
in Moscow 1984/85"

9. Appeal Chairman's Report ("Annex B")

" . . .

Alfred Kinzel:

Chairman of the commission of appeal World Championship 1984/85

re: Decision of the FIDE-President relating to the ending of the World Championship on February 15th, 1985.

My personal position

I was not only chairman of the commission of appeal, but I was representing the FIDE-President, Mr. Campomanes, in the course of his frequent absences from Moscow (Chess Olympiad Saloniki int. al.) exceeding two months as acting as leading authority of the World Championship.
So I had inevitably deep insights into the events of organisation and tournaments in Moscow.
Yesterday I came back from Moscow to Berlin. The German Chess Federation was so kind to give me instantly a documentation of more than 30 national and international press articles concerning the ending of the event. This night I studied the statements made in these articles and I arrived at the following conclusion: These conceptions and opinions made far from the site of decision and often made casually and explosively induce me to give a statement of facts to the public.
Hereby I am attached to certain agreed confidences concerning some points, but I will try to give a clear evidence.

Decisive proceeding

Late in January, the plan matured within the FIDE-President to delimit the marathon event by an agreement.

The plan provided that:

17

— Limitation of the event to 8 additional games
— in case of no decision within this time
— new competition in September with 24 games
— on a score of 0:0.

On February 1st, Mr. Campomanes invited both players to discuss this plan in common. Mr. Karpov came and agreed with the plan. Mr. Kasparov didn't come, but toward half past one a.m. his delegate, Mr. Mamedow.

Mr. Mamedow said that Mr. Kasparov wanted to continue the game.

Mr. Campomanes had to leave at the same morning toward 7 o'clock to take part in conferences in Switzerland, Greece, Israel and the United Arab Emirates.

Before his departure, he entrusted me with his representation and informed me of the result of his conferences.

I very soon understood that Mr. Mamedow could not make a compulsory for his player without consulting him.

Therefore I discussed once more all details of the plan with Mr. Mamedow. He was surprised of the details and promised to inform Mr. Kasparov and to obtain his final decision.

Mr. Kasparov's decision (he called it condition) was:
"I only agree with the plan if there will be no other games, but the event immediately ended at the mentioned conditions.
(Annotation: Score 5:2 for Karpov)

At the following period I had separate discussions with both player and their delegates. (Last: toward two hours each)
Mr. Karpov refused the conditions of his opponent (immediate ending of the game).

In virtue of the new ending-situation instead of limiting the event I tried for days to reach the FIDE-President in order to inform him of the changed situation.

I contrived to reach him and Mr. Campomanes immediately interrupted his travel, returned to Moscow and took over the pursuit of the discussions.

Mr. Campomanes who always proceeded from a limitation of the event was surprised and pleased with Mr. Kasparov's condition, that was to end immediately the event under the named conditions.

His main request was to surmount, from Monday to Thursday on the decisive week, the rejection and aversion of Mr. Karpov to an immediate ending.

Finally the FIDE-President was successful.

After a pause of reflection, both players made additional observations concerning the basic plan and made requests which are confidential. They led to an aggravation of the situation. Mr. Campomanes was not willing to fulfil these requests.

He decided, even without agreement to the players, to decide on his own by virtue of his office as leading authority of the World Championship.

This decision is – point by point – the condition made by Mr. Kasparov in front of the chief arbiter, Mr. Gligoric and myself, concerning the ending of the game.

Both players appeared at the press conference and declared "wanting to continue the game". Mr. Campomanes interrupted the conference and tried in another discussion of two hours to obtain a mutual written agreement of the two men. After fail, the following conclusions:

Mr. Karpov (hesitating) "I agree with the decision" and

Mr. Kasparov "I comply and I shall not protest".   . . . "

Here the official documents end.

THREE

Campo's Whistle-Stop

London (April)

After the distribution of the circular letter, Campomanes went on a whistle-stop tour of various FIDE member federations to explain his decision in person. The press conference in London was typical of this tour. It was hosted by publishers B.T.Batsford. Presiding was Batsford's chairman Alex Cox, while the audience consisted of leading British chess officials and members of the chess press.

Much had been written and broadcast about his decision without the benefit of Campomanes' own insights and he did, indeed, make a number of new points. He insisted, for example, that it was Svetozar Gligorić, the Chief Arbiter, who telephoned so urgently to Dubai, not a member of Karpov's camp, and that Gligorić was acting on the initiative of Alfred Kinzel, the FIDE representative in Moscow. He further maintained that in prior negotiations Kasparov himself had suggested halting the match and that Karpov was the first to demand a continuation. He pointed out that the public was wearying of the match after five months and 48 games and that the play of both contestants had seriously deteriorated and was no longer worthy of a world title match.

Accompanying the conference was a FIDE document containing Kinzel's own report to the world body, which backed up the majority of this. What elicited the most sympathy from the audience, however, was Campomanes's assertion that his decision to terminate had been agonisingly difficult and whatever he had decided he would have been severely criticised.

All this, we are sure, is true, but it proceeds from the arguable premise that a 'decision' was necessary at all. In fact, no decision was necessary since the match was proceeding according to regulations and these should have been allowed to run their natural course.

Having perused Kinzel's documents and listened to Campo first hand, we believed that this was the turn of events.

After Karpov lost game 47 Campomanes suggested to both players that the match be limited to a further eight games. If neither player could achieve the six wins required, then the match should be scrapped and a rematch scheduled later in the year. It was this action which, by creating a climate for a negotiated end, set the ball rolling for the eventual termination.

Karpov agreed, but Kasparov declined. Indeed, he would have been insane to accept such terms. With the score at 5-2 against him he could scarcely score his necessary four wins within an eight game period. Meanwhile the World Champion would have eight more opportunities to try anything and everything to notch his final and decisive victory, and could even lose three of them in his no-holds-barred onslaughts, without genuine risk of losing the match as a whole. Kasparov countered, understandably, with the argument that if the match had reached deadlock, it should be stopped at once. So much for Kasparov being first in wishing to halt the match.

True enough, Karpov was the first to demand in public that the match be continued, but only after his further suggestion that the match be suspended for a rest had been rejected and when he realised that the rematch would start at 0-0, not with the champion retaining a two-point advantage. Given his resolve to do 'something', Campomanes deserves real credit for resisting such suggestions which would have ridiculously favoured the World Champion. With this background, and assuming that it was Kinzel behind the Dubai call, we still find it difficult to believe that his activity was unprompted, either by a subconscious desire to save Karpov from sudden collapse, or by the USSR Chess Federation or by an element in the World Champion's camp. The theme for discussion in Dubai, after the call, was certainly 'Karpov cannot continue'. In fact, as co-author Keene entered the President's room in Dubai after the Moscow call, Campomanes greeted him with those exact words. The President was, however, later to state that this was "a conjecture, not a statement of fact".

What about public boredom, length of match, quality of play? After game 46 the public might well have been frustrated, but hardly after game 48, when Kasparov's sudden resurgence was hitting world headlines. Ironically, had Campomanes kept silent after game 48 and only stepped in to stop the match if there had been a further series of draws, his action would probably have met with widespread approval. It was halting proceedings just as Kasparov had won two in a row that aroused so much suspicion and hostility. The length of the match was five months, but as John Nunn pointed out at the conference, although 48 games is a world title record, it is not at all unusual for grandmasters to play 48 games over a five month period. And many of the Moscow games were very short and not at all strenuous. Finally, Karpov's play at the end was certainly no worse than Kasparov's at the beginning of the match, and quality of play cannot possibly constitute grounds for termination. Here, for example, are three positions from the 1951 Botvinnik-Bronstein match, generally regarded as one of the best and hardest fought of the series. Karpov-Kasparov at no stage touched such depths of ineptitude, and Bob Wade, who was representing FIDE in Moscow during the Botvinnik-Bronstein match as acting Vice-President, would have been hurled from the Kremlin's battlements by angry fans if he had tried to terminate that match even after these three egregious blunders.

21

Bronstein-Botvinnik, game 6

White, to play, thought for 45 minutes and played **57 ♔c2??** and **resigned** after **57 ... ♔g3**, when the e-pawn queens. Of course, 57 ♘e6+ and ♘d4 leaves Black fighting for the draw.

Botvinnik-Bronstein, game 9

White, a rook up for nothing, failed to win this game!

Botvinnik-Bronstein, game 17

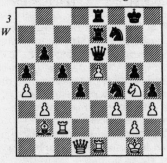

White blundered away a piece with **35 ♘f6+?** allowing **35 ... ♕xf6!**.

22

Immediately after returning from his whistle-stop tour Campomanes issued the following circular letter:
" . . .
President's Circular Letter No. 5, 1984/85.
25 April 1985

President visits the Americas.

I have just returned from a month long visit to the Western Hemisphere covering eleven national federations of Spain, Argentina, Chile, Paraguay, Bolivia, Ecuador, Peru, Colombia, Panama, Cuba, Mexico. The conditions under which these federations work have to be seen at close hand to be appreciated well. There was great enthusiasm for chess everywhere and I hope that FIDE's work in the region will be extended, if need be, with CACDEC support.

I took the opportunity to consult with officials of five other federations en route (USA, England, Ireland, Scotland and France). I regret that due to routing problems I had to by-pass some federations, especially in the Caribbean area.

Parenthetically, may I point out that during this tour, the Karpov-Kasparov match finale provided, without exception, the focus for media conferences organized by the federations.

Then and there, I realized the damaging extent of inaccurate information relative to my February 15 decision as relayed by media agencies to western Europe and to the Americas. I had occasion to examine in detail these reports that tended to obscure the facts as they occurred in the Sports Hotel on February 15.

Also, I noted outright distortions of facts from sources within chess circles. There appears to have been a pattern of disinformation.

I shall not now belabour this point. The proper forum is the Executive Council and the General Assembly. I shall then tackle this point by point, as I did in the media chess conferences in Latin America and the United States.

I started every meeting by distributing my Circular Letter (No. 4) dated 11 March, with its annexes. Then I took on all questions until there were none.

I am happy to say that 95% of these conferences ended in resounding and prolonged applause, especially that held at the Mexican National Council of Sports in Mexico City and that at the Marshall Chess Club in New York City.

Could this indicate that after the exposition of facts as they truly occurred, I had managed to disabuse the minds of people who earlier took a critical view because they based their conclusions on reporting that was at variance with the facts?

I worry not of the distorters and maligners. Daily, they have to look at their own images in the mirror. I am confident that truth will surface in the end.

Florencio Campomanes, President"

FOUR

Bidding High

London-Lucerne-Tunis (April/May)

At the end of April the British Chess Federation took what for it was a historic step. They submitted a bid in opposition to Moscow and Marseilles for the World Championship rematch. However, it was not to be. Co-author David Goodman wrote this report in the *Spectator* of 8 June:
" . . .

The decision of 29 May by FIDE President Campomanes to stage the whole of the Karpov-Kasparov rematch in Moscow brought to an end weeks of speculation about the playing site. The choice disappointed Western chess fans, many of whom had hoped to see at least part of the championship in Marseilles or London. However, what must not be forgotten is that the British Chess Federation's achievement of submitting a bid at all has greatly increased London's chances of holding a world title match in the future.

The BCF's offer was made possible by the staunch work of Martin Keen, managing director of Keen Media, a PR firm based in St Albans. The sackful of letters he sent to potential sponsors finally paid off on 30 April when the Greater London Council offered a prize fund of £300,000 to hold the match in London – just in time for Raymond Keene, in overall charge of the BCF's world championship campaign, to commission me to rush off to FIDE HQ in Lucerne to lodge the bid by the next day's noon deadline. I arrived in Lucerne with 45 minutes to spare to drop the envelope on Campomanes' desk.

Apart from Campomanes' familiar and almost mandatory attacks on Western press coverage of his decision to terminate the match in Moscow, his meeting with representatives from Marseilles and myself was good-humoured. Interestingly, the Marseilles organisers seemed to believe they would win a straight Moscow v Marseilles face-off and although offering the largest prize fund of around £500,000 they were obviously disappointed to see a bid from western Europe's leading chess capital.

On 6 May, Ray Keene flew to Tunis to lobby the FIDE Executive Council. Meanwhile, Stewart Reuben (the BCF's most experienced organiser) mobilised his considerable expertise to seek out possible playing halls, finally alighting on two impressive locations: Central Westminster Hall and the Queen Elizabeth Hall. Campomanes arrived in London on 21 May after his inspection trip to Marseilles and met Peter

Pitt and Ian McNicol of the GLC to discuss the sponsorship in detail. His trip to London was generously funded by Mobil North Sea.

In the event, after his subsequent visit to Moscow, Campomanes chose the Soviet Union for the entire match. The precise venue will be Moscow's Tchaikovsky Hall, so this time the demise of dignitaries or important political meetings cannot possibly interfere with the playing schedule. Campomanes' decision goes against the Executive Council's recommendation that Marseilles alone be considered the first alternative, with Marseilles-Moscow in second place and London-Marseilles split as the third. Moscow alone came only fourth. Another decision that will prove controversial is FIDE's imposition of a tax on the prize fund whereby FIDE itself now receives, for each draw, one per cent of the total prize fund in the forthcoming 24-game match. This could prove to be a considerable sum of money given that the Soviet Chess Federation was forced to equal the Marseilles prize bid of £500,000.

The one excellent decision to come from Tunis was that future title matches should be 'organised by different federations'. Given the amiable flexibility and effectiveness of the GLC and the possibility of locating new sponsors, things could go well for London. Not only will there be a title match in 1986, but should Kasparov win in September FIDE rules stipulate Karpov's right to a revenge match almost immediately. Thus, there is a possibility of two world championship matches being held outside the Soviet Union in the next 18 months . . . "

After the FIDE Executive Council had met during the Tunis Interzonal in May Campomanes despatched the following letter:

" . . .

President's Circular Letter No. 6, 1984/85.   14 July 1985.
MATCH FOR MOSCOW
The World Championship Match regulations entrust the President with the responsibility for choosing the Administrator and the venue for the match according to his evaluation of the following criteria: –
— the interest of FIDE
— the conditions
— the publicity prospect
— the wishes of the players
— the benefit of chess throughout the world . . .

The Council . . . recommended that France should have the first priority; next, that the match should be shared between France and the USSR; next, that the match should be shared between France and England; next, that the match should be held in the USSR; next, that the match should be shared between France, England and the USSR. In each of these alternatives the financial conditions should be those approved by Council.

Meanwhile, World Champion Anatoly Karpov had declared his preference for Moscow and Challenger Garry Kasparov had said he

25

preferred a venue in the USSR.

I visited the proposed venues in Marseilles, London and Moscow . . .

. . . after exhaustive consideration, I decided after consultations with Executive Council members, to name the USSR Chess Federation as the Administrator of the Match which shall take place in Moscow with the first game starting on September 2nd . . .

The important task of the Tunis Executive Council was to amend the World Championship Match Regulations . . . In essence, the amendments changed the "Conditions of Victory" in the following way:

(1) a win scores one point, a draw scores half-a-point;

(2) the player who wins six games wins the match;

(3) otherwise, the player who wins more games within 24 games, or who scores 12.5 points, wins the match.

(4) In the case that the score reaches 12-12, the World Champion retains the title.

(5) If the World Champion loses the match, there shall be no Return Match.

The above regulations are applicable to future World Championship Matches with the exception of the 1985 Karpov-Kasparov World Championship Match. For the 1985 Match the Council made the following "transitional" regulations applicable to the 1985 match:

(1) In the case of the 1985 World Championship Match, if the World Champion loses the match there shall be a Return Match.

(2) If this Return Match is played, the loser of the Return Match shall qualify, not for the Candidates' Semi-final Matches, but for a special Candidates' Final Tournament of 24 rounds with the winners of the Semi-final Matches.

This means that if the World Champion loses the 1985 Match, thus requiring a Return Match to be held, there will be four qualifiers from the Candidates' Tournament, not three, for the Candidates' Semi-final Matches. If a Return Match is not required, then the present Regulations for the Candidates' competition are applicable.*

Of special interest, perhaps, are the new regulations for division of the prize-fund. Noting that the number of draws in the recent World Championship Match attracted adverse comment, the Executive Council ruled that:

(1) for each game that he wins, a player will be paid 5% of the prize fund;

(2) for each game that he draws, a player will be paid 1% of the prize fund;

(3) for each drawn game, FIDE will be paid 1% of the prize fund for the CACDEC Fund;

(4) after deducting the above, the remainder of the prize fund will be divided, five-eighths to the winner and three-eighths to the loser . . .

F.Campomanes, FIDE President"

* *I.e. three would qualify. This decision, which meant the Candidates would not know how many of their number would qualify, was reversed at Graz.*

26

FIVE

Kasparov Strikes Back

Hamburg and Belgrade (May and June)

By the end of May Kasparov was determined to demonstrate his chessboard virility by playing well-publicised matches against Hübner and Andersson. Kasparov's score against Hübner constituted a marvellous victory, while his games looked like Alekhine and Capablanca rolled into one.

Hamburg, May-June 1985

Kasparov	1	1	½	1	½	½	4½
Hübner	0	0	½	0	½	½	1½

Hübner-Kasparov (1) *English Opening.* **1 c4 e5 2 ♘c3 d6 3 d4 ed 4 ♕xd4 ♘f6 5 g3 ♘c6 6 ♕d2 ♗e6 7 ♘d5 ♗e5 8 b3 ♘e4 9 ♕e3 ♘c5!**. Improving on the standard 9 ... c6. **10 ♗b2 c6 11 ♘f4 ♘g4 12 ♕d4 ♘e4!!**

A thunderbolt which leaves White stunned. If now 13 ♕xe4 ♕a5+ 14 ♔d1 ♘xf2+, or 13 ♘d3 f5! threatening ... c5. Finally, 13 ♘h3 ♕a5+ 14 ♔d1 d5 is horrible for White. **13 ♗h3 ♕a5+ 14 ♔f1 ♘gxf2 15 ♗xe6 fe 16 ♘xe6 ♔d7 17 ♘h3**. White's defence is resourceful, but ultimately useless. **17 ... ♘xh3 18 ♕xe4 ♖e8 19 ♘c5+ ♕xc5 20 ♕g4+ ♔c7 21 ♕xh3 ♗e7 22 ♗xg7 ♖hf8+! 23 ♗xf8 ♖xf8+ 24 ♔e1 ♕f2+ 25 ♔d1 ♕d4+ 26 ♔c2 ♕e4+ 27 ♔d2 ♗g5+ 28 ♔c3 ♕e5+ 0-1**

27

Kasparov-Hübner (2) *Queen's Gambit Declined.* **1 d4 ♘f6 2 c4 e6 3 ♘f3 d5 4 ♘c3 ♗e7 5 ♗g5 0-0 6 ♕c2 ♘e4 7 ♗xe7 ♕xe7 8 e3 ♘xc3 9 ♕xc3 b6 10 cd ed 11 b4 c6 12 ♖c1 ♗b7 13 ♗d3 ♘d7 14 ♖b1 ♕d8 15 0-0 a5 16 a3 ab 17 ab g6 18 ♘d2 ♕e7 19 e4.** Dramatically altering the nature of the pawn structure. Kasparov shows great confidence in his ability to whip up a kingside attack in exchange for the weakness of his d4 pawn. **19 ... de 20 ♗xe4 ♖ac8 21 ♖fe1 ♕d8 22 ♘c4 ♘f6 23 ♗f3 ♘d5 24 ♕d2 ♗a6 25 ♘e5 ♗b5 26 ♖ec1 ♕d6 27 h4 ♖fd8 28 h5 ♘e7 29 ♖e1 ♖c7 30 ♗g4 ♘d5 31 hg hg 32 ♖b3 f5 33 ♗d1 ♖g7 34 ♖h3 ♕xb4.** With both players in time trouble, Kasparov now sacrifices a rook to launch a mating attack. **35 ♕h6 ♕xe1+ 36 ♔h2**

36 ... ♔f8 37 ♘xg6+ ♔g8 38 ♕h8+ ♔f7 39 ♕xd8 1-0

Away from the board, Kasparov displayed great self-confidence, beating his chest and uttering Tarzanic ululations in denunciation of the powers which called off the earlier match, and amongst these powers he clearly numbered Karpov. His first unprecedentedly outspoken statements appeared in the pages of match sponsor *Der Spiegel* in the issue of 3 June 1985. The interview was entitled "At The End Karpov Was Scared" and subtitled "*Spiegel* talks with Challenger Kasparov concerning his chances of becoming World Champion". The interviewer was Editor Werner Harenberg and it took place in the Spiegel House in Hamburg. Here is an extract.

. . .

KASPAROV: At the moment there is no world chess champion. There has never been an end to a world chess championship such as the one in Moscow on 15 February, and hopefully there will never again be one in the future. In my opinion, after such an end to the struggle, Karpov has forfeited his right to call himself the world champion. On the other hand, I haven't yet earned this right since that can only be done by victories at the chessboard. This achievement still lies in the future for me.

DER SPIEGEL: You said when the match was terminated you had a 30% chance to win the world title. Weren't your chances better?

KASPAROV: I just happened to name that figure. Since then, Karpov often refers to it more or less like this: if Kasparov himself names 30%, then 70% is left over for me. However, you must take this into account. Before the last two games, my chances for a match victory were slightly better than zero. Now they suddenly shot up to 30%. That was a terrible fright for Karpov which totally paralysed him, since a third still meant a real chance of winning for me. But whether the number was correct is difficult to estimate. Actually it's irrelevant. Karpov either did not want, or was not able, to continue the match.

DER SPIEGEL: If that was the case, shouldn't he, from a sporting point of view, have resigned?

KASPAROV: For Karpov the word sport is an empty concept, just noise and smoke, while it's my opinion that we are playing for the whole world and can't just play around as we like. Karpov views the title World Champion as a natural prefix to his surname: "World Champion Karpov". He can't imagine it any other way.

After the 48th game, which was also the last, ex-world champion Botvinnik said to me: there are three variations in which the match can end. The first variation is the most unlikely: Karpov wins one game and the match ends. The second variation , Kasparov wins three games, that is already a bit more likely. The third variation is this: that the match is broken off. This is the most likely variation since the second is more likely than the first.

DER SPIEGEL: Botvinnik turned out to be right. Herr Kinzel, the former President of the West German Chess Federation, represented President Campomanes for some time in Moscow. At the close, he expressed himself in public, but only told half the truth, that half which was favourable to Karpov. We would like to hear from you the other half of the truth, or even the whole truth.

KASPAROV: To tell the whole truth presumes that I know it, but I don't think I know everything.

DER SPIEGEL: There were negotiations about the termination and Kinzel says you were prepared to have an immediate close, but then you added extra demands, and he has to keep quiet about those.

KASPAROV: Demands were certainly put forward, but Herr Kinzel confuses everything. They were demands from Karpov, not from me. The gentlemen are now trying, on top of all this, to put forward the case as if there had already been negotiations about a termination for a long time, as if negotiations had already started up in December. But it was not the way the gentlemen say it was.

DER SPIEGEL: Who are these gentlemen?

KASPAROV: Well, above all, the President of the World Chess Federation Campomanes and Karpov, the two friends, but also Kinzel and also, unfortunately, the Chief Arbiter, Mr Gligoric.

. . .Of course, Karpov has great influence. His two victories over Korchnoi have great political significance, but one still should not overestimate his capacity. He didn't succeed in holding me up on my way to a title match in the world championship. Now, in our country, where so many things are to be decided, the political leadership has worries other than chess. Karpov's people in the chess federation still seem to hold all the trumps in their hand, but appearances are deceptive.

DER SPIEGEL: Now that we've illuminated the background, let's go back to the negotiations about the termination. These didn't start as early as Karpov's men, Mr Campomanes and co, say they did.

KASPAROV: I am convinced that for a long time Karpov believed in victory and that he even saw the end before his eyes. For example, a lecture had been scheduled on the result of the world championship match for the 29 January in the Polytechnic Museum in Moscow. I have retained the entry card I bought. I could have brought it to Hamburg and shown it to you. Everything was ready for this lecture, but then on 30 January, it suddenly became 5-2. Then the thought surfaced to end the match. Various ideas were developed to by-pass the rules in force.

On the night of 1 February Campomanes, in agreement with Karpov, suggested the match be limited to a further eight games. And if nobody had won by then, the match should start again in September with the score at 0-0.

DER SPIEGEL: For the eight games still to be played, Karpov would only have to bring the score to 6-2, but you could scarcely have brought it up to 5-6. You would have had to win every second game.

KASPAROV: Quite right. I couldn't accept the decision. I then asked: why eight more games? If Mr Campomanes wants to break off the match, then he should do it at once. Kinzel has turned this sentence upside down and made it appear as if I had personally suggested that the match should be ended. But I didn't make such a suggestion at all.

DER SPIEGEL: Could one not accept that you would have agreed to a termination if the match would be restarted with the score at 0-0?

KASPAROV: Indeed, at the commencement of the negotiations, I would have been prepared for a premature termination of the match if I had been treated as a partner of equal rights and acceptable conditions had been suggested. Neither of these was done. I had a quite natural wish to use the chance to emerge with honour from a match which had been so difficult, and which had brought such little success.

DER SPIEGEL: Which additional demands did Karpov make which prevented agreement?

KASPAROV: Karpov's suggestion, which Kinzel brought to me, contained the following points:

1) Kasparov concedes defeat.

2) The next match begins in September at 0-0 and lasts 24 games.

3) If Kasparov wins this match with a lead of not more than three

points, he gets the title of world champion up to 1 January 1986. On 1 January 1986, Karpov becomes world champion again and Kasparov the challenger again, since the latter has shown no superiority in two matches.

4) If Kasparov wins the next match with a lead of four points or more, he becomes world champion and is obliged to defend his title . . . and so on.

DER SPIEGEL: Enough of this rubbish. This suggestion isn't worth the paper it's written on. Now it's very easy to understand why Herr Kinzel declared this to be confidential.

KASPAROV: I asked Herr Kinzel if he did not consider this suggestion to be an insult. He answered that I should think carefully about the suggestion, since the next match could be abroad and there would be a much higher prize fund.

DER SPIEGEL: Just as if injustice could be made good by money. But did Kinzel say anything about the reasons for the termination?

KASPAROV: He said, both players were tired. I happened to be one of those players and had to reply to him that this did not apply in my case and that, in fact, I felt significantly better now than at the beginning of the match. Kinzel then said something very important. There should be no separate negotiations between Karpov and myself. Everything had to happen under the aegis of FIDE. I then answered: I await Mr Karpov in the Hotel Sport at the chessboard and there under the aegis of FIDE we can clear up all questions. For that we need no Mr Campomanes and no Mr Kinzel, we just need a board with sixteen white pieces and sixteen black ones.

DER SPIEGEL: How did the conversation end?

KASPAROV: We spoke for a very, very long time. Kinzel tried ages to persuade me. It was very unpleasant for me as a young person to have to speak to a more elderly gentleman in this sharp form. Right at the end of the conversation I said the following, and this is very important: from this moment on I refuse absolutely to discuss any suggestion whatsoever from you.

DER SPIEGEL: Did your attitude to Karpov change?

KASPAROV: Considerably. Earlier on we had no problems, just a normal relationship, but that's a thing of the past. Karpov's suggestion which Kinzel brought to me and his further behaviour were an insult.

DER SPIEGEL: As ex-world champion Spassky says, Karpov would have to pay you one thousand dollars for a post mortem after each game so, as it were, he could look into your brain. Will this happen in the future?

KASPAROV: No, that won't happen in the future. Attentive observers saw that we already stopped doing it after the 48th game.

DER SPIEGEL: Have the rules which will be in force for the match starting on 2 September been discussed with the players?

KASPAROV: They have not been discussed with me, and with Karpov

31

they didn't need to be discussed, since they are simply in accordance with his own suggestions.

DER SPIEGEL: Have you also made suggestions?

KASPAROV: Yes.

DER SPIEGEL: Where were they published?

KASPAROV: Nowhere.

DER SPIEGEL: What have the sets of suggestions got in common?

KASPAROV: Nothing.

DER SPIEGEL: According to Karpov and FIDE, the match will be between the world champion and the challenger. According to you there is, at the present time, no world champion. What function do you give Karpov and yourself?

KASPAROV: The players are the world champion from 1975-84 and the victor of the qualifying cycle from 1982-84.

DER SPIEGEL: According to Karpov and FIDE 24 games will be played. If the match reaches 12-12, Karpov retains his title. What was your suggestion?

KASPAROV: My idea was to play 24 games and if 12-12 is reached another six should be played. If it's still level, Karpov should receive the title of world champion. Please note that he should *receive* it and that only after 30 games. While according to his suggestion, he would *retain* it and that only after 24 games.

DER SPIEGEL: According to Karpov and FIDE, if Karpov loses he gets the right to a return match. What was your suggestion?

KASPAROV: I did not envisage a revenge match.

. . .

DER SPIEGEL: Let's assume that Karpov and his friend Campomanes, whom Spassky, since the termination of the world championship match, refers to as "Karpomanes", follows the schedule and lets the title match start on 2 September, give us a tip – how will the match end?

KASPAROV: I'm absolutely determined to show my full strength in such a struggle. It is difficult to defeat Karpov, but I believe I have good chances to do it. I'm only not in a position to defeat Karpomanes.

DER SPIEGEL: Mr Kasparov, we thank you for this conversation.

Here the inverview ends. The translation from German is by co-author Ray Keene. Extracts of the English language translation originally appeared in *Chess Life*, September 1985.

Having demolished Hübner in Hamburg, Gary Kasparov went on to Belgrade to face the Scandinavian grandmaster Ulf Andersson. Andersson, it will be remembered, played on top board for an international team in last year's historic USSR-World match in London Docklands. He is one of the toughest players to beat, and in this respect his style approximates closely to that of Hübner and Karpov himself.

Kasparov's choice of locations and opponents for his matches was, however, motivated by considerations other than the latters' stylistic similarity to the World Champion. The two officials who had most strongly supported the FIDE account of events at the end of the Moscow match were the German Kinzel and the Yugoslav Gligorić, respectively Jury Chairman and Chief Arbiter. Significantly, Kasparov selected the home countries of these two to contest his matches, and he wasted no time in making his opinion of their actions totally clear.

Meanwhile, in an interview in *New in Chess*, former world champion Boris Spassky weighed in with some penetrating assertions of his own: "After Karpov had accepted the decision of Campomanes to terminate, which was an incredible thing to do, he found himself in an extremely unpleasant situation. He was the only one who had not foreseen that in the ensuing situation he should have taken care of his prestige in the first place. Karpov experienced irreparable bad luck – but it was all his own fault. As far as Campomanes is concerned, by his decision . . . he actually destroyed Karpov."

At this time, too, Gligorić and Kinzel were reappointed for the September rematch, a questionable move by FIDE since Kasparov was evidently in public dispute with them both and could have little confidence in their impartiality.

Belgrade, June 1985

Kasparov	½	½	1	½	1	½	4
Andersson	½	½	0	½	0	½	2

Kasparov-Andersson (3) *Catalan Opening.* **1 d4 ♘f6 2 c4 e6 3 g3 d5 4 ♗g2 dc 5 ♘f3 c5 6 0-0 ♘c6 7 ♘e5 ♗d7 8 ♘a3 cd 9 ♘axc4 ♘d5.** Varying from 9 ... ♖c8 which he had tried earlier. But Andersson's new idea actually seems less convincing. **10 ♘xc6 ♗xc6 11 ♕xd4 ♘b4 12 ♗xc6+ ♘xc6 13 ♕c3 f6.** An unpleasant weakening, but otherwise he cannot develop his king's bishop. **14 ♗e3 ♗e7 15 ♖fd1 ♕c7 16 ♕b3!.** A fine move which pinpoints Black's vulnerable points at b7 and e6. **16 ... g5.** Another horrible move, but if 16 ... 0-0 17 ♘d6! ♗xd6 18 ♕xe6+ winning material. **17 ♖ac1 ♖d8 18 ♖xd8+ ♗xd8 19 ♕xb7!.**

33

A neat combination which nets a vital pawn. **19 ... ♕xb7 20 ♘d6+ ♔d7 21 ♘xb7 ♗b6 22 ♘c5+ ♗xc5 23 ♗xc5 f5 24 ♖d1+ ♔c7 25 ♖d6 ♖e8 26 b4 a6 27 fe h5 28 h4 gh 29 gh ♖g8+ 30 ♔f2 ♖g6 31 a4 f4 32 b5 ab 33 ab ♘e7 34 ♖a6 ♘f5.** Even Andersson's fabled powers of resistance cannot make much of a fight of this ending. **35 ♖a7+ ♔c8 36 b6 ♖g7 37 ♖a4 ♔b7 38 ♖xf4 ♔c6 39 ♖c4 ♔b5 40 ♖b4+ 1-0.** 40 ... ♔xc5 41 b7 ♔xb4 42 b8♕+ wins.

The main contribution to the debate during the Andersson match occurred in the form of an exchange of open letters between Gligorić and Kasparov. Here, first, is Gligorić's letter, published on Sunday 16 June in *Politika*, a major Yugoslav newspaper. Bear in mind that Gligorić at that time still considered himself eligible for the neutral post of Chief Arbiter.

" . . .

I am sorry I could not welcome you when you came, unexpected for me, to Belgrade. I am glad that you are a guest in the city where I was born and that my club, Partizan, for which I started playing 15 years before you were born, is your host. My club omitted to let me know that your visit had been included into its 40th anniversary, although I am the President of the Celebration Board.

You had 4 months to announce what you thought about my refereeing, and I was aghast at the absence of good taste with you if you could choose such place and time for your 'discovery' of the disappearance of some of my virtues after Feb. 1st this year! You are introducing some new style into public interpersonal relations./.../ Your interpretations have formed a picture about the match I intimately knew did not correspond to the real course of events. That caused a lot of undeserved annoyances for me when I came back home. Even the main editor of 'Sahovski Glasnik' in Zagreb, possibly cheered up by your thesis, stowed me, in his highfaluting commentary, into the 'FIDE bureaucracy' that had prevented you, 'by Karpov's order', to win the match./.../

The decision of the president of the FIDE, announced to the world on Feb. 15th, was identical with your own proposal.* I could not understand your protests, and your terming of that decision, which defended your interests, too, as 'dirty'. You accuse me for not having been against it. Why should I? As a referee, I had no such right. I do not blame the former world-champion Botvinnik for stating that my duty was to protect the rule-book of the match. Botvinnik probably presupposes that chess is played today as it used to be thirty years ago, when the president of FIDE only closed the match and the referee had an easy task both because of the sportsman-like characteristics of the opponents, as well for the fact that he knew the exact date of the

* *Gligoric, too, suffers from the same arithmetical confusion as Kinzel, namely that the score of 5-2 is somehow identical with 5-3! (see page 44)*

beginning and closing of the match.

But, according to the current Book of Rules, proclaimed by the FIDE chess congress after the unpleasant experience with the match in Baguio, the only supreme authority in the world championship match is the FIDE president himself. A referee is an expert who commands inside the so-called 'playing zone' while a game is in progress. About everything else FIDE president decides by himself. I stuck to my role as prescribed.* For five months, I used to see Karpov and you on the stage only. I never proposed anything to you, I never visited you, nor did I even know where you were staying. My only contact with you was by phone, after Feb. 1st, when attempts began to find a solution for the marathon match by players' agreement. /.../

Yes, but you have a 'trump-card' in Feb. 13th, when 'Gligoric came with Campomanes' / why not – Campomanes with Gligoric? What is the important role that you ascribe to me? / with 'the intention to persuade' you to agree with the proposal that the match be broken up. what an acrobatic feat is that? My visit was accidental. FIDE president surprised me asking me to accompany him. I phoned to your headquarters, explained the situation, told that I did not wish to come, but if it is considered at your side that it might be of some help, I would come. The answer of the chief of your staff was positive. You forget that Campomanes and you were talking most of the time at the table while I was sitting on a sofa with Mamedov a few meters away, waiting optionally until we went away. /.../

You assert that 'Gligoric did his best to accept Campomanes' proposal' that the match be stopped. You are mixing up the past events again. When I spoke for the first and the last time, it was at that 'closed conference' – the question was not about Campomanes' proposal anymore, but about the announced final decision, when the sharpness of your reaction made the atmosphere yet heavier. This is not the place for me to explain what I did in my sincere wish that the spirits be appeased post festum. /.../

And finally, your heaviest accusation – that I was fanning for Karpov. I know myself a hundred times better, and partiality is the last thing that can happen to me. Curiously enough, after such an assertion of yours, I stopped taking seriously anything that you might say except on the chessboard . . .

S.Gligoric"

* *FIDE President Campomanes has repeatedly stated that the phone call to Dubai on 9 February was made by Gligorić. This statement is supported by US FIDE Delegate Don Schultz, who was in the room with Campomanes at the time. Phoning Dubai seems inconsistent with commanding inside the playing zone .*

Kasparov had earlier made this comment on the subject of Gligorić's role: "When I have – behind closed doors – in the recess of the Feb 15 press conference, demanded play to be continued, Gligorić was the first to say: it is out of the question, the match will not be continued!" He now replied to Gligorić's open letter with his own, given here in translation:

Honoured GM Gligorić,
The letter you have addressed to me is discouraging. Responding to my concrete objections with respect to the role you had assumed by the end of the match, you wrote an article which I would characterise as strange, if not insulting!

Before your article appeared in the press, you stated that the facts speak against me. Nevertheless, one cannot find such facts in your article. Instead, you state the fact that you have begun playing for the chess club 'Partizan', which organised my match with Andersson, fifteen years before I was born. The use of such arguments is not exactly a sign of good taste.

You also criticise the former world champion Botvinnik for commenting on the events on the basis of his experience from thirty years ago. In other words Botvinnik is, according to you, too old to keep up with the times, and I myself am too young to understand things in the right manner. What, then, should we make of Boris Spassky, who in contrast to Botvinnik was not informed about the strange events which took place at the end of the match, but nevertheless shared the same opinion?

I would like to repeat once more that I never had anything against you personally. Moreover, as you know well, you were my first candidate for the position of referee before the match with Karpov began. As I had stated earlier, I made this decision because I considered you one of the most esteemed gentlemen in the chess world. I would like to state that this was not only my opinion. Your unquestioned reputation in Yugoslavia, as well as in the whole world, is well deserved.

However, we are all men, Grandmaster Gligorić, and even the best of us sometimes make mistakes. To my great sorrow, you made a series of serious mistakes in Moscow. More than four months after the match you are still unaware of the fact that you were only a cog in Campomanes' machine, although that probably was not your intention. This fact, however, cannot be changed anymore. Your attempt to interpret the events that took place in the last days of the match for your own purposes convinced me that it is necessary to inform the Yugoslav public about the true state of affairs; only in this way can people in your country get the correct picture of what happened.

In the other FIDE report, as well as in the interviews you gave immediately after the match, you characterised Campomanes' decision as right and just. Many people from all over the world, as well as in

Yugoslavia, criticised you because of this statement. Do you still hold to that opinion? If you do, then please explain why it was necessary to break off the match in such a way? Do you not think that it was your obligation as a referee, and even more importantly as a grandmaster, to see to it that the outcome of the world championship was decided on the chessboard? If you do not share this opinion, what is it that makes you different from those FIDE bureaucrats who invent and interpret the rules in the way that suits them best?

It is true that I kept quiet for four months, hoping that the next match would be played on an equal basis, and that not all of my proposals would be ignored, which nevertheless happened. This means that the match will be played once more in Moscow (I suggested that it be played in any other city in the USSR, for example in Leningrad), which is Karpov's place of residence. I live in Baku.

During the last four months, I have become aware of the fact that it is possible to stand in the way of Campomanes' intrigues only by informing the public about the true course of events which took place at the time of the last match.

You are perfectly right in saying that I greatly contributed to the anxious atmosphere in which the closed meeting took place. True, this was my fault; but this was so because I was the only one who wanted to continue the match. Everyone else – Campomanes, Kinzel, Sevastianov and you – stated that it was impossible to continue the match. As for Karpov, he, as you remember, immediately signed Campomanes' decision about the termination of the match.

Beginning on February 1st, the day of my victory in the 47th game, three different proposals about the breaking-off of the match were made. This is well known to you, by the way, but two of the three proposals you never even mention, for some reason. You state that the match was stopped with my consent. I think that this statement of yours deserves no further comments. Instead, let us try to remember the three proposals:

Campomanes' proposal on 1 February: "Eight more games should be played, and if the match is not decided, a new one will be played in September, the starting score being 0-0".

Responding to that proposal I said that I did not understand why the match should be played at all, if the rules are being changed. But let us forget that statement. At the beginning of the negotiations I had really given my consent; I accepted the idea of temporarily ending the match under the condition that I be treated as an equal partner, and that some reasonable proposals be offered to me. I hope that as a chessplayer you understand that I wanted to end this complicated and complex match in a dignified manner.

As you remember, I told you the same thing at the time. After that, I waited for Karpov's proposals the whole day. Finally, Kinzel brought them to me on 4 February. Here they are:

a) Kasparov accepts that he lost the match.

37

b) A new match will be played in September, the score 0-0 being the starting point. If Kasparov wins the match with a 3-point advantage or less, he will be the world champion until 1 January 1986.(!) After that Karpov regains the title and Kasparov can play in the matches for the world championship. If Kasparov wins with four or more points advantage, he becomes the world champion and is obliged to defend his title at a tournament of three players (in 1986) – against Karpov and the winner of this round of qualifying tournaments.

Kinzel accepted these propositions in the name of FIDE, although this amounted to breaking all FIDE rules about the competition for the world championship. I hope that you have not forgotten your attempts to convince me, on the phone, "to carefully consider these proposals". You know equally well of my response to Kinzel: "I consider Karpov's proposals personally insulting, and from now on reject any proposal for breaking off the match". By the way, what do you think about Karpov's proposal from a professional standpoint?

After that Campomanes submitted a new proposal on the night of 11-12 February. At that time I had won the third game and the score was 5-3. There is no need to reconsider all his proposals in detail. Let us stick to the first and most important point.

"The match will be played until the 60th game." This tells us that on his arrival in Moscow Campomanes had not yet made the decision to interrupt the match. However, the letter of the President of the Soviet Chess Federation, Sevastianov, in which he asks for a three-month break because of the exhaustion of the players, appeared soon afterwards.

Campomanes and you (and not you and Campomanes, as I mistakenly said before) came to me on 14 February. The heads of my delegation, two seconds and the translator were also present at the meeting. You showed Sevastianov's letter to me, and we reconsidered the situation. I would like to stress that you took active part in these serious negotiations. From time to time you even helped the translator, who did not have a clear idea of all the details.

During the talks I clearly and categorically stated that I saw two ways of ending the match. First, Karpov should resign the match if he is not capable of continuing it. Second, we will continue the match till the end according to the present rules.

Campomanes responded by saying there was yet a third possibility: "he alone would make the decision". What these threatening words meant I found out the next day, 15 February, at the press conference.

This was the last in the series of strange events which were not exactly in the spirit of the game of chess. A good example is provided by the technical time-outs of the organisers and the President of FIDE. Has the chess world seen anything like this before this match?

Campomanes' shocking decision caused a wave of protest on the part of world chess opinion. Everyone, from grandmaster to casual chess fan, asked themselves how it was possible to break off a sports competition on somebody's order. Only a small group of people, closely connected with the FIDE leadership, supported this unpopular decision. To my great sorrow, you were among them.

It is not, therefore, surprising that you were sharply criticised in Yugoslavia. You should not as a result be trying to blame me for what happened. Every man has to take responsiblity for his actions.

You are trying to present my efforts to protect my rights, as well as the interests of chess, as an attempt to put psychological pressure on Karpov. All my matches, including the match with Karpov until the 47th game, were characterised by fair play. I can add, without even a single case of protest.

Obviously, you have not even noticed that you are repeating Kinzel's and Sevastianov's formulations in your letter: "Kasparov is so exhausted that he cannot even comprehend it". But whereas they said that on 15 February you are repeating the phrase four months later; in the meantime I have played two matches – against Hübner and Andersson.

The chess world is going through hard times. A battle for the purity of the ideals of chess is taking place. It is hard to believe that such a renowned player as you is on the wrong side. Campomanes and his company are not at all interested in the infinite beauty of the game of chess, but you are a true chessplayer and I am convinced that you are not indifferent to the fate of this game. This is not the right company for you, Grandmaster.

I am sorry that this letter will draw your attention away from chess. However, I was forced to read your article and write a response during my match with Andersson.

This match was as important to me as the tournament which you are participating in is to you.

Gary Kasparov

SIX

Karpov's Defence

Amsterdam (July)

Karpov had been reticent in expressing his own opinion but, on the eve of the match, he defended himself in an extensive interview in *Vrije Nederland* given to journalist Max Pam and grandmaster Genna Sosonko. This was during the OHRA tournament, which Karpov won convincingly – his answer to Kasparov's matches against Hübner and Andersson.

This extract contains the most important points made by Karpov.

" . . .
There was no conspiracy between Campomanes and myself. In fact I had not expected his decision to stop the match. I met him the night before his 15 February press conference and pointed out that a termination was only acceptable for me in the form of a two-or three-month break: why should I throw away a lead of two points? The following day I spoke to Campomanes in our sport committee building. He was considering stopping the match at 5-3 without declaring a winner, but I dismissed this as nonsense and preferred to play on rather than face those conditions. 'O.K.', said Campo, 'but then you must play game 49 today.' I thought this ridiculous. I had been feeling nervous the whole preceding night, I had woken up at 9 a.m., instead of midday which is usual for me in a match, and on top of that I hadn't prepared at all for the game. 'If that's the case, then I'll play,' I said, and set off for my dacha, 15 kilometres outside Moscow, to get ready for the game. In my car I suddenly heard from a friend via my 'mobilophone' that Campomanes had taken a definite decision. Campomanes had mounted the podium, declared that he had three possibilities, but that God (sic) had inspired him to stop the match. I was shocked, sped back to the press conference, but came too late. Until the moment I came, Kasparov had said nothing about continuing. Stopping the match was, of course, a dream result for him, so when he did get up to speak he always used the past tense: 'Mr President – you knew my position . . . that I wanted to continue . . .', not 'I want to continue'. When the three of us adjourned for a private discussion, I did something incredibly stupid, in that I was the first to sign Campomanes's document terminating the match. Kasparov then refused to sign and said: 'I submit to the decision but I'm not signing what Campomanes has ordained.' This gave the impression that I was eager to stop, but he wasn't . . . Some days later, after my open letter

demanding resumption, Campomanes and Gligorić tried to contact Kasparov, but they only came up against his mother and helpers, who insisted on speaking only in Azerbaijani.   ... "

Is it in fact possible that Karpov's meeting with Campomanes ended in a huge misunderstanding, Campomanes believing that Karpov had refused to play that day, while Karpov thought he had agreed to play that afternoon?

OHRA, Amsterdam, July 1985

		1	2	3	4	5	6	
1	Karpov	● ●	½ ½	1 1	1 ½	½ ½	1 ½	7
2	Timman	½ ½	● ●	½ ½	0 1	1 1	½ 1	6½
3	Nunn	0 0	½ ½	● ●	½ ½	½ 1	1 1	5½
4	Miles	0 ½	1 0	½ ½	● ●	1 0	½ ½	4½
5	Martinović	½ ½	0 0	½ 0	0 1	● ●	½ ½	3½
6	Sunye Neto	0 ½	½ 0	0 0	½ ½	½ ½	● ●	3

Karpov's wins with White against the English grandmasters Nunn and Miles were particularly subtle:

Karpov-Nunn. *Sicilian Defence.* **1 e4 c5 2 ♘f3 d6 3 d4 cd 4 ♘xd4 ♘f6 5 ♘c3 a6 6 ♗e2 e5 7 ♘b3 ♗e7 8 0-0 0-0 9 ♗e3 ♗e6 10 ♕d2 ♘bd7 11 a4 ♖c8 12 a5 ♕c7 13 ♖fd1 ♖fd8.** With the tactical point that 14 f3?! d5! 15 ed ♘xd5 16 ♘xd5 ♗xd5 17 ♕xd5 ♘f6 18 ♕c4 leads to equality. However, Karpov played **14 ♕e1!?** and there followed **14 ... ♕c6 15 ♗f3 ♗c4?**, which does nothing to inhibit White's plan, and after **16 ♘c1 h6 17 ♘1a2 ♘c5 18 ♘b4 ♕e8 19 g3 ♖c7 20 ♗g2 ♖dc8 21 b3 ♗e6 22 ♘cd5 ♘xd5 23 ♘xd5 ♗xd5 24 ♖xd5** White had a clear plus:

The finish was efficiently handled by Karpov: **24 ... ♖c6 25 ♖ad1 ♘e6 26 c4 ♗g5 27 ♗a7! ♖a8 28 ♗b6 ♗d8 29 ♗e3 ♗c7 30 ♕e2 b6 31 b4! ba 32 b5 ab 33 cb ♖c5 34 ♗xc5 ♘xc5 35 ♗f1 a4 36 ♕c2 a3 37 ♗c4 ♘e6 38 ♖5d3 ♘d4 39 ♕a2 ♗b6 40 ♖xa3 Black lost on time**.

The brief comments are based on those by John Nunn in the September 1985 issue of the *British Chess Magazine.*

Karpov-Miles

It is hard to believe that White could win this thematic Caro-Kann ending. **48 f4 g6 49 hg fg 50 ♔d4 h5 51 ♔e4 ♔f7 52 ♖b3 b6?**. Safer is 52 ... ♖b8. **53 ♖d3 ♔e7 54 ♖d6 bc?**. Better 54 ... ♖c8. **55 ♖xc6 ♖b8 56 ♖xc5 ♖xb2 57 ♖c7+ ♔f8 58 ♖xa7 ♖c2 59 ♔f3 ♔g8 60 a4 ♖a2 61 a5 ♔f8 62 a6 ♔g8 63 ♖a8+ ♔g7 64 a7 ♖a3+ 65 ♔e4** and **Black resigned**. White brings his king to the queen's side and then heads for e6.

SEVEN

Arbitrary!

Graz (August)

During early August further details emerged on the vexed question of officials for the September rematch. Campomanes had indeed reappointed Kinzel as Jury Chairman and Gligorić as Chief Arbiter, even though both were heavily implicated in the termination of the previous match and, consequently, in open, written and flagrant dispute with Kasparov.

In a sharp retort Kasparov announced that he would not play the next match at all if Gligorić were to accept the arbiter post. Indeed, according to regulations, the Chief Arbiter should be on the list of preferences submitted by both players. The only person to fit this bill was the highly respected German grandmaster Lothar Schmid, who had officiated at the Fischer-Spassky match of 1972 and Korchnoi-Karpov in 1978.

Kinzel attempted, in a rambling document of self-justification sent to various FIDE officials, to defend himself against Kasparov's *Der Spiegel* allegations. We here reproduce a translation of it in full.

" . . .

In *Der Spiegel* of June 3 1985 I am mentioned by name eleven times. The impression given of myself, of FIDE President Florencio Campomanes and of the Chief Arbiter of the match, GM Svetozar Gligorić, is that of a group of FIDE functionaries attempting to hinder Gary Kasparov from reaching his goal in life – the title of world chess champion. The technique used to create this impression was for *Spiegel* editor Werner Harenberg to ask Mr Kasparov several leading questions designed to put us in the wrong.

When I returned to Berlin from Moscow on February 19, I read through some thirty articles from the national and international press concerning the cancellation of the championship match. Their gist was that President Campomanes' decision to cancel the match worked to Mr Kasparov's disadvantage. Such words as "manipulation" and "play-acting" were common.

The theory generally advanced was that the President caved in to the requests of the Soviet sports leadership which, it was held, preferred the Russian Karpov to the Armenian Jew, Mr Kasparov (formerly Weinstein). It was this nonsense which prompted my initial public statement about the real events during the final stage of the world championship.

43

What, then, really happened from February 1 to 15?

On 1 February the FIDE President proposed limiting the match to a further eight games. To the surprise of all concerned, Kasparov only wanted to accept this proposal if the match was halted immediately. This suggestion of Kasparov was absolutely identical with the FIDE President's decision of 15 February. If you take this into account, on 15 February Kasparov received from Campomanes everything he had demanded at the start of February.* This shows that his decision was not made on the spur of the moment but matured over a two-week period.

My dealings with Werner Harenberg began when I presented my statement of fact to him on 20 February. He requested an interview with me, but I would agree to this only upon prior publication of my statement in *Der Spiegel*. His reply that he would have to make further investigations seemed inadequate, since the press had already published untrue statements without any investigation. As I see it, the *Spiegel* interview with Kasparov is a sort of continuation of my meeting with Mr Harenberg. So let us look at the specific points raised in this interview to see how valid they are.

First, are FIDE functionaries trying to prevent Mr Kasparov from becoming world champion? Where, one asks, is the proof? My view is that Messrs Karpov and Kasparov have both enhanced the prestige of chess. FIDE trusts both of them, considers their interests and acts for the welfare of both gentlemen.

Secondly, was it a violation of the rules to cancel the match? President Campomanes' decisions were based upon FIDE regulations, and the Executive Council of FIDE at its May 1985 meeting in Tunisia approved unanimously Campomanes' decision to cancel the match, thanking him for his initiative.

The next charge is that I twisted one of Mr Kasparov's sentences to suggest that he wanted to end the match. Yet the fact remains that the conditions stipulated by Mr Kasparov are identical to those enunciated by Mr Campomanes when he ended the match. To wit: the match would end immediately, without an additional eight games.

Did I, as Mr Kasparov alleges, exert pressure on him to accept Mr Karpov's offer? Personally, I did not agree with Mr Karpov's proposal, and I so told Mr Karpov. He replied that it was only a basis for discussion. I duly informed the Challenger of the

---

* *This line of reasoning is open to doubt since by 15 February the score had altered to 5-3 and Kasparov had won two games in a row. In* New in Chess *Timman provided the most elegant demolition of Kinzel's fallacious argument: "Campomanes agreed to Kasparov's proposal after the situation in the match had clearly changed, as the score was no longer 5-2 but 5-3. This can be compared to a person who first rejects an offered draw and then, a few moves later when his position has deteriorated considerably, wants to accept it after all."*

proposition, and I never tried to persuade him to accept it. As for the advantages and disadvantages that I discussed with Mr Kasparov, those familiar with international negotiations know that intermediaries ask questions to establish a basis for compromise.

Mr Kasparov mentions my injunction that there be no separate negotiations between the two players. My real point was that one should try to come to a common solution in a circle of three persons (Mr Campomanes or myself and the two players). I was merely trying to attempt once more what the FIDE President tried earlier – to get the two players together. The President's attempt failed because Mr Kasparov did not appear.

Then there is the unpleasant and false implication contained in Mr Harenberg's remark, "now it's very easy to understand why Mr Kinzel declared this to be confidential." He was referring to Mr Karpov's plan to end the match. In reality, there were two things that Mr Campomanes declared to be confidential: the Champion's proposition and a certain request that Mr Kasparov made. The motive was to protect the two players. Mr Kasparov made public Mr Karpov's offer, but I feel bound to remain silent about Mr Kasparov's even stranger request. This is because FIDE is not a forum for washing linen in public.

What emerges is that the reasons advanced by the press for the cancellation of the match are untrue and that the charges against FIDE must crumble away. The *Der Spiegel* interview is an attempt to obscure my position and to distort what actually happened.

It is a fruitless attempt using transparent means.

Alfred Kinzel, Chairman of the Match Jury"

We are reliably informed by an authoritative source that the "even stranger request" consisted of the following: a) Karpov should renounce his world title, and b) declare that he was at the end of his physical resources, as preconditions for halting the match. Which set of proposals was the stranger, Karpov's initial set or Kasparov's rejoinder, we leave the reader to judge for himself.

The prevailing atmosphere of the FIDE Congress at Graz which finished on 31 August, a few days before the start of the world championship, was one of exhaustion and demoralisation. The irregularities committed by the Federation's leadership over the past eight months had exerted an enervating effect on the delegates.

FIDE's main blunders this year have been: the termination of the 1984-85 world championship, the appalling complications of the hasty new Candidates' regulations from Tunisia, and the suspect reselection of Gligorić and Kinzel as match officials. Fortunately, the more sensible elements of the Graz Congress did succeed in unravelling the Candidates' confusion (by deciding that four should qualify whoever won the

45

world championship match), and Gligorić did resign as Chief Arbiter. This paved the way for the choice of Malchev (Bulgaria) and Mikenas (Lithuania) as joint umpires with Prins (Holland) and Vachessar (Estonia) as deputies.

Nevertheless, the Arbiter situation was only resolved in the final minutes of the last full session. Meanwhile, the following telex was speeding from Gary Kasparov, and it arrived just too late for general distribution.

" . . .

Statement to all delegates of FIDE:

Once more I'm forced to protest against the numerous errors and obvious provocations committed by Campomanes and his people in arranging the forthcoming title match between me and Karpov. To have no chief arbiter just three days before such an event is another unprecedented scandal. Since Mr S.Gligorić has withdrawn, as is well known, in early July, there was plenty of time to replace him, for instance by Mr Lothar Schmid who was in both players' lists. He was ready to take the job too, only needing a written invitation in good time, being a businessman. Instead, Campomanes phoned him only a few days before the Congress on 19 August. At that time he knew perfectly well that Mr Schmid would no longer be able to accept the invitation. This is Campomanes's false alibi, so he might have another so-called 'extra-ordinary case', when he can use his presidential power to act as a dictator. Campomanes's general approach is wrong in many ways. He is violating moral principles and written rules daily. By the way, I have replied to all letters from the President, but, apparently, my replies get mysteriously lost. Isn't it strange?

His ignoring of all my requests puts me in a handicapped situation. Serving, however – opposite to the President – the chess world's best interest, I feel obliged to play even under such conditions. I only hope that the fate of the world championship title will be decided on the chessboard – this time.   . . . "

There is evidence to support Kasparov's claim that Schmid was frozen out by FIDE's refusal to acknowledge that Gligorić had stepped down. At a press conference in Belgrade on 25 July a statement from Gligorić was read out by the President of the Yugoslav Chess Federation: Gligorić, having considered his position, and not wanting to be seen as an impediment to anyone's (i.e. Kasparov's) chances, had withdrawn from the post of Chief Arbiter. However, on 6 August Lim Kok Ann (FIDE General Secretary) telexed the British Chess Federation as follows:
" . . .
WCCM CHIEF ARBITER S GLICORIC (CORR. GLIGORIC), DEPUTY ARBITERS, Y AVERBACH AND V MIKENAS. FIDE HAS NOT BE NOTIFIED OF ANY PROPOSED CONTRARY. REGARDS LIMKOKANN GENERAL SECRETARY"

EIGHT

On the Eve of the Match
September

A key factor in the psychological armoury of every reigning champion is self-belief. Once this is damaged, the seeds of defeat may be sown for the next challenge. Karpov has adopted two stances in quick succession on the decision by the President of FIDE to terminate the last match. At the final press conference he acquiesced, then within two days he had altered his line to implacable opposition and demanded, via an open letter to Reuters, that the championship be continued. It is, however, difficult to believe that a Soviet world champion, leading by five wins to three, requiring one more win for outright victory, and playing in his home city of Moscow, could not have insisted on an immediate continuation if that had truly been his desire.

Most players would be depressed by this bizarre acceptance to withdraw from a situation two games ahead and would be commensurately affected. But, as proved at Baguio in 1978, Karpov has immense resilience and ability to bounce back, and a surprising capacity to suppress standard emotions.

Stylistically Karpov, like Capablanca, is essentially a repressive player, one who rarely loses and whose forte is the neutralisation of any possible adversarial advantage. Whereas this technique has sometimes degenerated into sterility, Karpov combines it with a fierce killer-instinct over the board.

For this coming challenge Kasparov, whose approach to chess is basically a revolutionary one, should have learnt to play a waiting game. As the last match progressed, he curbed his desire to launch unclear sacrificial attacks (as he did in games 2 and 6) and saved the fireworks until his opponent had been strategically outplayed and the position was ripe for a combinational explosion. This is the vital lesson Kasparov has to learn from his hero, Alekhine – and it was the only way in which Alekhine finally ground down Karpov's prototype, the super-solid Capablanca, in their world title contest at Buenos Aires in 1927.

What of Karpov's stamina? This could be of importance in the match about to start, but it should be remembered that this has now been limited to 24 games by FIDE, so stamina may never arise as an important question.

Indeed, the rule changes implemented by FIDE have left Karpov in the most insulated situation of any world champion since the series commenced in 1886. Karpov has not only been protected by FIDE from the effects of his apparent collapse in the previous match, he has reclaimed the odds of the draw and will retain the title if the score is 12-12. Karpov also has the right to a revenge match within three months if he should lose. But this right has been abolished for all future champions!

In an analysis for *The Times*, David Spanier, chess journalist and former diplomatic correspondent of that paper, addressed himself to the political dimension. In the two Korchnoi-Karpov clashes of 1978 and 1981 the political tensions between orthodox Soviet citizen and vociferous defector were more than obvious. In the current match they are more subtle, pointing rather to recent realignments of political balance within the USSR after the accession to power of Mikhail Gorbachev.

"The rise to power of the new Soviet leader Mr Mikhail Gorbachev has been the signal for a rapid clearing out of the old guard in the Kremlin. New men and new ideas are coming in. It would be surprising if this flurry of activity did not also cover the single most important sporting-cum-cultural activity in the Soviet Union: chess. The world championship match which opens in Moscow on Tuesday [3 September], therefore, will be more than a test of skill over the board . . .

Mr Gorbachev may not concern himself directly with chess; Kasparov himself may not think in such political terms. But it has not escaped notice that one of the faster rising members of the Politburo, Mr Geidar Aliev, comes from Azerbaidjan. He is reputed to be a supporter of Kasparov. Influence in high places is no bad thing in the Soviet Union. In any case, if young Kasparov is to make good his words, if he is to survive and prosper, he had better play well."

Other experts have supported this broad view. In the *Financial Times* of 14 September, Z.A.B.Zeman argued that with the rise to power of Mr Gorbachev the focus of power and concern was shifting away from European Russia to the regions:

"The roots of Andropov and Gorbachev lay elsewhere – which is why with the latter's elevation to the Kremlin the centre of gravity of Soviet power is shifting and changing the Politburo's composition. The Stavropol region (Gorbachev's home area) is part of the south-eastern marshlands of Russia. Georgia, Armenia and Azerbaidjan lie close to the south, with the central Asian republics beyond the Caspian Sea. The steppe arches over the Black and Caspian Seas, linking central Asia to the Ukraine.

From the Andropov-Gorbachev viewpoint, neither European Russia nor the Ukraine can present Moscow with political surprises. The success or failure of Soviet rule will be determined in Asia and in Siberia . . .

The area of greatest opportunity marches with the area of most severe problems. This fact has made its impact on the Politburo. Mr Gorbachev is following in the direction marked out by Andropov. The latter's drive against corruption opened in Azerbaidjan, where the party and government leadership was dismissed in 1969. (The operation was directed by the local KGB head, Mr Geidar Aliev. He became candidate member of the Politburo in 1976, a full member under Andropov in 1982.) . . .

The West will have to respond to more than a new style of leadership. Personal changes in Moscow, so far, and the underlying shifts in the centres of gravity in the Soviet Union, will become gradually reflected in its domestic and foreign policies. The pace will become faster and Western leaders will have to keep up with it."

The chessboard struggle between Karpov and Kasparov may be the tangible symbol of the growing challenge of the regions of the USSR (represented by the Jewish-Armenian Kasparov from Azerbaidjan) to European Russia, from which Karpov comes.

"It might be that, as Gorbachev creates a new style of leadership, articulate, urbane, decisive, the young man from Baku is set to become part of the new image of itself that the Soviet Union wants to present to the outside world."

Dominic Lawson, Financial Times

GAME ONE, 3 September

At the opening ceremony on 2 September, where Soviet Culture Minister Pytor Demichev presided, Campomanes spoke of FIDE as a "human organisation" and continued: "We had the most unusual competition last time around . . . I hope that the players, their assistants, match officials and FIDE have gained from our experience last time". He described February's events as "in the past" and in an effort to defuse the 'Fidegate Scandal'* said, "I wish good luck to both players". This point was echoed by co-Chief Arbiter Andrei Malchev (Bulgaria), who said: "I respect the two players equally". Chess fans who packed the 1,500 seat Tchaikovsky Hall – where the famous music competition is held – applauded both Karpov and Kasparov. But Kasparov hardly applauded Campomanes when he spoke – he just put his hands together two or three times – and Karpov and Kasparov did not shake hands. There was no mention of Kasparov's appeal to FIDE sent to Graz.

One Russian aide said: "It doesn't seem like six months. For three months we discussed the decision, then for two we discussed the prospects for a new match". There was cheering when Kasparov drew the white pieces for game 1.

"Another casting of lots, rather unusual, was also held to determine who of the two chief judges will head the panel of judges on alternative days. Mikenas will head the judges on odd days. Naturally, he will supervise the first game on 3 September. The opening ceremony was attended by guests of honour – representatives of the chess communities of Australia, Brazil, Indonesia, France, Yugoslavia, as well as FIFA President Joao Havelange, in the USSR in connection with the World Youth Football Competition." – Novosti

* The term used by US Chess Federation magazine Chess Life to describe events surrounding the termination of the previous match.

50

We have seen no Kasparov interviews in the Soviet press, but a number from Karpov. On Monday 2 September in the Moscow evening paper *Vechernyaya Moskva*, Karpov praised Kasparov's victories over Hübner and Andersson as "deserved . . . His advantage in the openings was especially noticeable". Novosti, referring to this interview, also quoted Karpov as stating that International Grandmasters Igor Zaitsev and Sergei Makarichev would be his official seconds in the match and as naming International Grandmasters Yefim Geller and Yevgeny Vasyukov among his assistants.

For the first game two thousand eager fans waited expectantly by the police cordon placed around Mayakovsky square, in front of the Tchaikovsky Hall. Campomanes arrived first – twenty minutes before play. Then Kasparov, twelve minutes before, with two of his seconds, Dorfman and Timoshchenko.* Klara Kasparova, Gary's mother, came in a second later. With only seven minutes to go, another car came through the cordon, but it was an official one with flags. Karpov's car with his head of delegation, Baturinsky, arrived only about three minutes before the game and play began a little late.

Kasparov made his entrance on the stage first, shook hands with the arbiters and went to the board. When Karpov followed, applause seemed about equal. There was a formal, but quick and perfunctory handshake.

Kasparov's 3 ♘c3 was clearly a surprise and Karpov spent around 45 minutes on his first five moves. The World Champion was soon in obvious difficulties after his mishandling of the unusual opening variation – a wry comment on Karpov's own indirect praise of Kasparov's expert handling of this department of the game. After a queen exchange White exerted a horrific cramp on the World Champion's position, which rapidly resulted in White's gaining a pawn, without relaxing his grip.

Cumulative times, in minutes, are shown after each move. Players have 150 minutes each for their first 40 moves and 60 minutes per 16 moves thereafter.

Kasparov-Karpov
Nimzo-Indian Defence

| 1 | d4 | 2 | ♘f6 | 0 |
| 2 | c4 | 3 | e6 | 0 |

3 ♘c3 4

Already a surprise, since this sharp move was totally avoided in their previous match, preference being given to 3 g3 or 3 ♘f3.

* *Nikitin is Kasparov's other second and Zayev is his head of delegation. Mamedov, the previous head of delegation, is now his press spokesman.*

3	...		♗b4	2
4	♘f3	4	c5	18
5	g3	4		

And this is highly unusual. It is based on an idea of Alekhine, Kasparov's hero, but the former champion favoured the move order 4 g3 to combat the Nimzo-Indian, e.g. 4 ... d5 5 ♗g2 0-0 6 ♘f3 c5, as in Alekhine-Golombek, Margate 1938.

| 5 | ... | | ♘e4 | 47 |

Alternatively 5 ... ♗xc3+ 6 bc ♕a5 7 ♕d3 ♘e4 8 ♗d2 f5 9 ♗g2 ♘c6 10 d5 ♘d8 11 0-0 ♘f7 12 ♖fd1 0-0 13 a4 d6 14 ♗e1 ♕a6 15 a5 ♗d7 16 ♘h4 ♖ae8 (0-1, 43) was Polugayevsky-Korchnoi, Linares 1985, but "Victor the Terrible" did not repeat this in their next clash! Polugayevsky-Korchnoi, Tilburg 1985, several months later, varied with 5 ... ♘c6 6 ♗g2 ♕a5 7 d5 ♗xc3+ 8 bc ♘e7 9 ♕d3 ed 10 cd ♘exd5 11 ♗d2 ♕a6 12 c4 ♘e7 13 e4 d5!? with great confusion, though Black also went on to win this one.

| 6 | ♕d3 | 4 |

6 ♗d2 has also been played, and appears to have been introduced in one particularly venerable game: Rubinstein-Maroczy, London 1922, continued 6 ... ♘xd2 7 ♕xd2 ♕a5 8 ♗g2 0-0 9 0-0 cd 10 ♘xd4 ♘c6 11 ♖ac1 ♕c5 12 ♘xc6 bc =. This idea was revived in Ubilava-Agzamov, USSR First League 1984: 6 ♗d2 ♘xd2 7 ♕xd2 cd 8 ♘xd4 ♘c6 9 ♗g2 ♘e5 10 ♘c2 ♘xc4 11 ♕d4 ♗xc3+ 12 ♕xc3 ♕a5 13 b4 ♕c7 14 ♖c1 d5 15 ♘a3 ♗d7 16 ♘xc4 dc 17 ♕xc4, also =.

| 6 | ... | | ♕a5 | 47 |

6 ... d5 is also respectable.

| 7 | ♕xe4 | 4 | ♗xc3+ | 47 |
| 8 | ♗d2 | 4 | | |

Of course, not 8 bc? ♕xc3+ and ... ♕xa1.

| 8 | ... | | ♗xd2+ | 47 |
| 9 | ♘xd2 | 4 | | |

Now Black has various possibilities, of which Karpov's choice is one of the least appetising:

a) 9 ... 0-0 10 dc ♘a6 11 ♗g2 ♘xc5 12 ♕e3 d5 13 b4! ♕xb4 14 ♖b1 d4 (14 ... ♕a5?? 15 ♖b5) 15 ♕xd4 ♕a3 16 0-0 ♕a5 17 ♘b3 ♘xb3 18 ab ♖d8 19 ♕e3 ±/±.

b) 9 ... cd 10 ♕xd4 0-0 11 ♗g2 ♘c6 12 ♕e3 d5 13 0-0 d4 14 ♕d3 ±.

c) 9 ... ♘c6!? 10 d5 ♘d4 11 ♔d1 or 11 ♗g2.

| 9 | ... | | ♕b6? | 56 |

Commencing an adventure with his queen which breaks all the

rules (do not move your queen around in the opening, do not take the b-pawn with your queen, etc).

10 dc *8*

Improving on the game Ubilava-Vishmanavin, USSR First League 1984, which saw 10 0-0-0 cd 11 ♘b3 ♕c6!. If now 10 ... ♕xc5 11 ♗g2 0-0 12 0-0 followed by ♘b3 and ♖fd1 with typical Catalan-style pressure against Black's somewhat retarded queen's wing.

10 ... **♕xb2** *57*

11 ♖b1 *8* **♕c3** *60*

After this Black is faced with a grave and permanent positional inferiority. 11 ... ♕xa2 fails to 12 ♕d4! 0-0 13 ♕c3. 11 ... ♕a3 was Ubilava-Lerner, USSR First League 1983. That game continued **12 ♗g2** ♕xc5 13 0-0 ♘c6 14 ♖fd1 with compensation, but **12 ♕d4** looks good. Interestingly, Ubilava and Lerner have worked with Karpov, so he should have known this game. Judging by the clock times, only Kasparov knew about it.

12 ♕d3! *12*

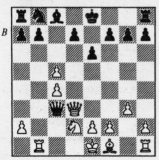

A fine move, forcing off queens and leaving Black permanently cramped and unable to develop his queenside forces.

12 ... **♕xd3** *78*

13 ed *12* **♘a6** *78*

14 d4 *30* **♖b8** *78*

Alternatively, 14 ... e5 15 de ♘xc5 16 ♗g2 ♘d3+ 17 ♔f1 with White still on top. 16 ... ♔e7 might be better. However, Karpov tries to free himself by steering for ... b6.

15 ♗g2 *35* **♔e7** *99*

If 15 ... b6 16 cb ab 17 ♔e2 ♗b7 18 ♗xb7 ♖xb7 19 c5 b5 20 ♘c4.

16 ♔e2 *40* **♖d8** *113*

17 ♘e4 *53* **b6** *113*

18 ♘d6 *56*

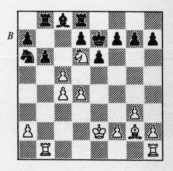

18 ... **♘c7** *115*

Abject retreat, but if 18 ... bc 19 ♖xb8 ♘xb8 20 dc ♘a6 21 ♘xc8+ ♖xc8 22 ♗b7 ♖xc5 23 ♗xa6 ♖a5 24 ♗b7 ♖xa2+ 25 ♔e3 ♖c2 26 ♖a1 should win.

19 ♖b4 *64* **♘e8** *127*

20 ♘xe8 *69*

After the game Dorfman was to claim that 20 ♘xc8+ might be even more accurate, since Karpov should now have played 20 ... ♖xe8!, keeping his king active on e7.

20	...		♔xe8	132
21	♖hb1	70	♗a6	133
22	♔e3	71	d5	140
23	cd6	81		

Even stronger than 23 cd5 followed by cb. Kasparov now switches his attention to hounding Black's exposed queen's bishop.

| 23 | ... | | ♖bc8 | 146 |

Or 23 ... ♖xd6 24 c5.

| 24 | ♔d3 | 84 | | |

Possibly stronger is 24 ♖a4 ♗xc4 25 ♗b7 b5 26 d7+, but there is certainly nothing wrong with Kasparov's continuation of the attack.

| 24 | ... | | ♖xd6 | 146 |
| 25 | ♖a4 | 84 | b5 | 146 |

Desperation and the only way to salvage the bishop.

| 26 | cb | 85 | ♖b8 | 146 |

Exploiting the pin restricts his losses to one pawn.

| 27 | ♖ab4 | 92 | | |

Another good line is 27 ♔e3 ♖xb5 28 ♖xa6 or 27 ... ♗xb5 28 ♖ab4 ♖db6 29 ♖xb5 and ♗c6+.

27	...		♗b7	146
28	♗xb7	93	♖xb7	146
29	a4	93	♔e7	149

Black's situation is still hopeless, since White's extra pawn and Q-side majority are bound to produce a winning passed pawn.

30	h4	100	h6	149
31	f3	105	♖d5	149
32	♖c1	106	♖bd7	149
33	a5	110	g5	149
34	hg	114	♖xg5	149
35	g4	114	h5	149
36	b6	115	ab	149
37	ab	115	♖b7	149
38	♖c5	116	f5	149
39	gh	118	♖xh5	149
40	♔c4	119	♖h8	149
41	♔b5	125	♖a8	149

Adjourned. Kasparov sealed.

| 42 | ♖bc4 | 151 | | |

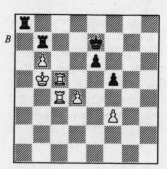

And **Karpov resigned**, not a moment too soon, e.g. 42 ... ♖ab8 43 ♖c7+ ♖xc7 44 ♖xc7+ ♔d6 45 ♖h7 f4 46 b7 ♔d5 47 ♖d7 mate.

This game represents Kasparov's third successive victory against the World Champion, if we include the two games he won in his late revival in the previous match, which was annulled. We can think of no one else who has won three consecutive games against Karpov.

The respected Soviet grandmaster Mark Taimanov wrote:

"A first game is always of a special kind: everything in it matters – the choice of opening, the pace and character of the struggle and, of course, its result. To some extent, it may also reflect the spirit and aspiration of the competitors, and divulge secrets of analytical preparation. The contest proved to be both interesting and spirited."

To the authors of this book, however, Karpov's play in game 1 did not look like any kind of improvement over his performance in game 48, the last one of their previous match.

During the game Karpov's board-side flag fell to half mast and stayed there till the end of the session. Many noticed the symbolism.

Karpov   0
Kasparov   1

Victory goes to the player who first scores six wins. If neither player manages this Kasparov's target is 12½ points and Karpov's 12, since Karpov is to retain his title in the event of a drawn match. As for the official "prize fund", it has been screwed up by FIDE to "1,600,000" Swiss Francs. This notional sum is simply the basis for a levy by FIDE on the USSR Chess Federation. The latter have already conceded 24% of it as a donation to CACDEC, the FIDE Commission for Developing Countries. This is even more generous than the 1% tax per draw originally conceived by FIDE at their Tunis gathering. The result is that FIDE will take almost 400,000 Swiss Francs for itself, vastly more than the players, since the actual *prize* fund has been estimated as 50,000 golden roubles, or only around 140,000 Swiss Francs.

GAME TWO, 5-6 September

"Kasparov took a 1½-½ lead over Karpov as they agreed their second game drawn in 65 moves. The first session of the game had been a thrilling tactical battle, but in adjournment play Karpov's accurate defence soon neutralised and captured Kasparov's dangerous passed pawns. At the end, neither grandmaster seemed willing to offer a draw in a level position, but finally they shook hands after Karpov's 65th move.

"Karpov supporters were pleased to see him break his streak of three losses against Kasparov, including two in the aborted challenge earlier this year, and experts praised the Champion's clinical defence after the turbulent complications of the first session. A Brazilian Chess Federation official described the game as "all-action, like our soccer team", while Soviet grandmasters called it the best the two had ever played together. However, one of Kasparov's aides declared that the Challenger should have won."

(Leonard Barden, in one of his excellent *Guardian* reports on the match)

The night before the second session Botvinnik predicted Kasparov's sealed move. The Kasparov camp had hoped to win the game and were disappointed with the result. In contrast, Karpov joked with spectators outside the Hall.

During the first session Campomanes walked through the press room and was overheard to say: "It looks like a draw". Good judgement or wishful thinking? At the end Karpov moved some pieces around as if to go for a post mortem, but Kasparov put on his jacket and abruptly marched out of the hall. So no post mortems, as Gary had indicated in his Yugoslav and *Spiegel* interviews.

Karpov-Kasparov
Sicilian Defence

(Loud applause for both players)

1	e4	1	c5	0
2	♘f3	1	d6	1
3	d4	1	cd	1
4	♘xd4	1	♘f6	1
5	♘c3	1	a6	2
6	♗e2	2	e6	2
7	0-0	2	♗e7	3
8	f4	5	0-0	3
9	♔h1	5	♕c7	4
10	a4	13		

This variation arose three times in the previous match. In the fifth game Karpov chose 10 ♗f3 but Kasparov had no trouble equalising after 10 ... ♘c6 11 a4 ♖e8 12 ♗e3 ♖b8 13 ♖e1 ♗d7 14 ♕d3 ♘xd4 15 ♗xd4 e5 16 ♗a7 ♖bc8 17 ♗e3 ♕c4 18 a5 h6 19 h3 ♗f8 20 ♗d2 ♕d4. Meanwhile, in the 43rd game Karpov could also achieve no success in gaining a tangible advantage with the continuation 10 ♕e1 b5 11 ♗f3 ♗b7 12 e5 ♘e8 13 f5 de 14 fe ♗xf3 15

ef+ ♖xf7 16 ♘xf3 ♘d7 17 ♗g5 ♗f8 18 a3 ♘d6 19 ♘d2 ♖xf1+ 20 ♕xf1 ♕c6 21 ♖e1 ♖e8.

10	...		♘c6	4
11	♗e3	13	♖e8	5
12	♗f3	14	♖b8	12
13	♕d2	16	♗d7	15

The opening had been the same as game 45 from the earlier match until Kasparov's intended home improvement over his choice then, 13 ... ♘xd4. Karpov now used up half an hour on his reply.

| 14 | ♕f2 | 49 | | |

We were amused by this magnificently committal comment by Matsukevich to Novosti: "During this time many well known grandmasters discussed a lot of different continuations".

In fact, only Maia Chiburdanidze succeeded in predicting Karpov's plan.

14	...		♘xd4	23
15	♗xd4	50	e5	24
16	♗e3	59	♗e6	57

Kasparov consumed more than half an hour on this amazingly risky move – one which seems to indicate, by inviting mind-boggling complications, that he was actually playing for a win with Black. Dorfman recommended 16 ... ef followed by ... ♗c6 or ... ♗e6 combined with ... ♘d7 as far safer.

17	f5	79	♗c4	70

No going back. If 17 ... ♗d7 18 g4! and Black will be swiftly rolled up on the king's flank.

The problem with Kasparov's move is that the bishop on c4 represents a highly attractive target which Karpov now tries to trap.

18 ♗b6 *81* **♕c8** *89*

The grandmasters now gathering in force in the press centre were rather expecting 18 ... ♕c6 19 ♖fc1 ♗d8.

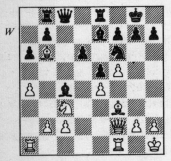

19 ♖fc1 *105*

White wants to play 20 b3, snaring the bishop, without permitting the tactical resource 20 ... ♗xb3 and ... ♕xc3. Therefore he bolsters up his c3 knight from the rear.

However, incredible as it may seem, Kasparov now conjures up a maze of obscure complications, and the general belief was that 19 ♖fd1 might have been an improvement. Some variations:

a) **19 ♖fd1** d5 20 ♘xd5 ♗xd5 21 ed ♗d6 and Black is fine. But 20 ed ♗b4 21 ♘e4 ♕xf5 22 ♘g3 ♕c8 23 d6 is good for White. Alternatively, 19 ♖fd1 d5 20 ed ♗b4 21 ♘e4

♕xf5 22 ♘xf6+ ♕xf6 23 b3 e4 24 bc ef or 22 ♘g3 ♕c8 23 b3 e4 24 ♗h5 e3 25 ♗xe3 ♗xd5 26 ♗a7 ♖a8 27 ♖xd5 ♖xa7 28 ♖g5.

b) **19 ♖fe1** d5 20 ed ♗b4 is obscure. If 20 ... ♕xf5 not 21 g4 ♘xg4 22 ♗xg4 ♕xg4 23 ♖e4 ♗d5, but 21 ♗c7!.

19 ... **d5** *96*

Evidently the only move. Black must activate his pieces in order to rescue the stranded bishop. The sequence up to move 25 is forced.

20	b3	*108*	♗b4	*97*
21	♘a2	*109*	♗a3	*98*
22	bc	*115*	♗xc1	*99*
23	♘xc1	*118*	♕xc4	*100*
24	ed	*118*	e4	*101*
25	♗e2	*119*	♕xc2	*104*
26	♕d4	*124*		

There were rumours in the press centre that Karpov thought 26 d6 immediately might be better.

26 ... **♖bc8** *122*

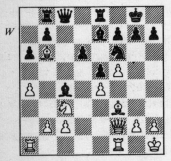

The critical position. Black's combination has actually led to a situation where he has nominal material equality – rook plus one pawn against two bishops. Furthermore, Black has a fairly dangerous passed e-pawn, White's pieces exhibit a certain disharmony and Black can well consider possible queen sacrifices on c1. The main drawback from Black's point of view is the colossal threat posed by White's own passed d-pawn, a threat enhanced by the fact that White's bishop on b6 controls the promotion square. Over the next few moves Karpov becomes confused and actually loses his passed pawn without eliminating its black counterpart. The question here is could White improve in this position? Some sample variations:

a) **27 d6**. This appears not to work, viz 27 ... ♛xc1+! 28 ♖xc1 ♖xc1+ 29 ♗d1 e3 30 d7 e2 31 de♛+ ♘xe8 and Black wins. The leitmotif is clear: back-rank pin and ruthless advance of the black passed pawn.

b) **27 ♗d1!** ♛xc1!? (27 ... ♛c4 28 ♛xc4 ♖xc4 29 ♗b3 ±) 28 ♖xc1 ♖xc1 and now:

b1) **29 ♛d2** ♖b1 30 ♗g1 (not 30 d6? e3 or 30 ♗e3 ♘g4) and:

b11) **30 ... e3** 31 ♛c2 ♘e4 32 ♗xe3 (not 32 ♛xb1? ♘f2+ 33 ♗xf2 ef and Black wins) 32 ... ♘c3 33 ♛xc3 ♖xd1+ 34 ♗g1 h5 35 d6 ♖ee1 36 ♛c8+ and 37 ♛c5 wins.

b12) **30 ... ♖ec8!** 31 d6 ♖cc1 32 d7 ♘xd7 33 ♛xd7 h6 34 ♛e8+ ♚h7 35 ♛xe4 f6 36 ♛g4 ♖xd1 37 ♛g7+

with a draw by perpetual check.

b2) **29 h3** e3 30 ♚h2 e2 31 ♗xe2 ♖xe2 32 ♛f4 ♖b1 33 ♛b8+ ♖e8 34 ♛xb7 ♘xd5 35 a5 ♘xb6 36 ab a5 37 ♛a7 h6 38 b7 (38 ♛xa5 ♖b8 =) 38 ... a4 39 ♛a8 ♖f8 followed by ... a3-a2 forcing a draw.

As readers can see, the position after 26 ... ♖bc8 is one of the most complex and fascinating ever to have arisen in a world title match. It is hardly surprising that Karpov tried to cut through this tangled jungle of variations with a quiet positional move to relieve his problems on the back rank. Nevertheless, the complicated 27 ♗d1! certainly deserved preference over the move for which Karpov now opts.

27	h3?	*125*	e3	*125*
28	d6	*138*	♛d2	*129*
29	♘d3	*141*		

The best move could be 29 ... ♘d7! 30 ♘f4 ♛xd4 (not 30 ... ♖c6 31 ♖d1) 31 ♗xd4 ♖e4 32 ♘d5 ♖c2 33 ♗d3 ♖xd4 34 ♘e7+ ♚f8 35 ♗xc2 ♖xd6 36 f6 g6 37 ♗b3

59

♘xf6 38 ♘c8 ♖c6 39 ♘a7 – unclear, but probably good for Black.

29	...		♕xe2	*131*
30	d7	*142*	♘xd7	*131*
31	♕xd7	*142*	♕d2	*133*
32	♖e1	*144*	e2	*134*

Kasparov may, perhaps, have missed the best on move 29, but he has still succeeded in destroying White's passed pawn while maintaining his own formidable e-pawn on an extremely menacing post.

33	♔g1	*144*	a5	*138*
34	g3	*147*		

Avoiding the trap 34 ♔f2? ♖cd8 35 ♗xd8 ♕e3 mate.

34	...		♕h6	*142*
35	♗f2	*148*		

If 35 ♗xa5 then 35 ... ♕e3+ and ... b6.

35	...		♕c6	*142*
36	♕xc6	*148*	♖xc6	*142*
37	♖b1	*149*	♖c4	*143*
38	♖xb7	*149*	♖xa4	*144*

The exchange of weaknesses on b7 and a4 has resulted in a second passed pawn for Black. It is the a-pawn, in fact, on which Kasparov must rely for his winning chances, since the pawn on e2, though fairly secure at the moment, is well and truly blockaded and has little chance of promotion.

39	♗e1	*149*	♖a3	*144*
40	♖d7	*149*		

If 40 ♘e5 then 40 ... ♖e3 attacking White's knight and following up with ... ♖f3-f1.

40	...		a4	*146*
41	♔f2	*149*	♖b3	*152*

The sealed move.

42	♘c1	*149*		

Karpov is said to have thought Kasparov missed a win on move 42, but this is not clear. 42 ... ♖b5 is the suggested move, but then 43 ♖a7 ♖xf5+ 44 ♔g2 ♖f1 45 ♘d3 g5 46 ♖xa4 ♖e3 47 ♖d4 ♖xd3 48 ♖xd3 ♖xe1 49 ♖e3 seems drawn as White plays h4 and ♔f2 and Black can only reach bishop's pawn and rook's pawn in the rook ending.

At resumption Karpov looked depressed. Perhaps he had mainly been devoting his attention to the line 43 g4 ♖a8 44 ♘a2 (44 ♘xe2 a3 45 ♗c3 a2 followed by ... ♖b1) 44 ... ♖b2 45 ♖d2 a3 46 ♔xe2 ♖d8 47 ♖xb2 ab 48 ♘c3 ♖c8! or 47 ♘c3 ♖dxd2+ 48 ♗xd2 a2.

42	...		♖b1	*155*
43	♘a2	*149*	♖a8?	*160*

This looks very weird. Did he miss White's next move?

44	♖e7	*162*	♖b2	*165*
45	♖xe2	*162*	♖xe2+	*165*

60

46	♔xe2	*162*	♖e8+	*166*
47	♔f2	*163*	h5	*167*

Dorfman says ... g5 was the best freeing move for Black.

48	♗c3	*164*	♖b8	*169*
49	♗b4	*164*	♖d8	*171*
50	♔e2	*173*	a3	*189*
51	♗c3	*177*	f6	*192*
52	♗b4	*191*	♔f7	*192*

In the ending Black's plan is to infiltrate the White position by playing his rook to c4. If Black did not need the h-file to infiltrate with his rook then 52 ... ♔h7 might be winning, as there is no knight fork on d6 to defend the f-pawn and White's h6 ideas become less dangerous in the future.

53	♘c3	*193*	♖b8	*193*
54	♘a2	*193*		

Naturally, Black's pawn is impervious here – 54 ♗xa3? ♖b3.

54	...		♖b5	*200*
55	g4	*194*	♖b8	*200*

The threat is 56 ... hg 57 hg ♖h8, intending to invade the second rank with decisive effect. Another attractive possibility is 55 ... ♖e5+ 56 ♔d3 ♖d5+.

56	♔d3	*201*	♖d8+	*201*
57	♔c4	*202*	♖d1	*202*
58	♗xa3	*221*	♖a1	*220*

"There was a lively discussion at the press centre of the move 58 ... h4, aimed at getting a passed pawn on the kingside. But in this case too White had enough defensive resources. For instance, 59 ♘c1 ♖h1 60 ♘d3 ♖xh3 61 ♗d6 and if 61 ... ♖f3 then 62 ♔d4, while if 61 ... ♖h1 then 62 ♔d4 h3 63 ♘f2. White must be vigilant now." — Taimanov

59	♔b3	*221*	♖h1	*220*
60	gh	*221*	♖xh3+	*221*
61	♘c3	*221*	♖f3	*223*

If 61 ... ♖xh5 62 ♘e4 indirectly protects White's pawn on f5.

62	♗c1	*222*	♖xf5	*224*
63	h6	*222*	g6	*234*

After 63 ... g5 there is also a neat tactical saving line: 64 ♘e4 ♔g6 65 h7 ♔xh7 66 ♘xf6+ ♖xf6 57 ♗xg5 with a theoretical draw.

64	♘e4	*222*	♖h5	*235*
65	♗b2	*224*	**Draw Agreed**

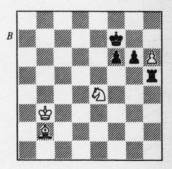

The variation runs: 65 ... f5 66 h7 ♖xh7 67 ♘g5+.

Karpov	0	½	½
Kasparov	1	½	1½

GAME THREE, 10 September

After his three-day rest, Karpov held an easy draw in game three. The Champion resorted to his favourite defence, the Queen's Gambit Declined, and after just 15 moves grandmaster experts were already predicting that the game would end in a draw.

Kasparov pondered for 36 minutes over his 16th move, ♗b1, in an attempt to align his queen and bishop for a mating attack against the black king. Karpov parried this efficiently enough with 17 ... g6 and Kasparov's subsequent breakthrough in the centre on move 18 merely led to an exchange of pieces and clear equality.

Karpov offered the draw, which was accepted. By this game the World Champion appears to have demonstrated that he has overcome the bout of nerves which adversely affected his play during the first two rounds.

Kasparov-Karpov
Queen's Gambit Declined

There was wild cheering and chanting from one section of the audience when Kasparov came to the stage. In contrast, Karpov's applause was more restrained.

1	d4	0	♘f6	0
2	c4	0	e6	0
3	♘f3	1	d5	2
4	♘c3	2	♗e7	3
5	♗g5	2	h6	3
6	♗xf6	8	♗xf6	3

7	♕b3	9

Kasparov had spent six minutes on 6 ♗xf6 and quickly played 7 ♕b3. 7 ♕d2 was games 19 and 21 and 7 e3 was game 27 of the previous match.

7	...	c6	31
8	e3	13

Another more aggressive continuation was analysed in the press centre, with Grandmaster Eddie Gufeld a particular protagonist: 8 0-0-0 ♘d7 9 e4 de 10 ♘xe4 0-0 11 g4. But, as Taimanov noted with a certain sarcasm, it is much easier to play like this in the press centre than on the stage.

| 8 | ... | | ♘d7 | 42 |

When asked if he had seen the position before Dorfman laughed, saying nothing. Then, " . . . Well, maybe this morning".

9	♖d1	16	0-0	46
10	♗d3	16	b6	51
11	cd	21	cd	55
12	e4	28	de	57
13	♗xe4	29	♖b8	57
14	0-0	32	b5	66
15	♖fe1	47		

Naturally, an immediate 15 d5 would have been countered by 15 ... ♘c5, though 15 ♗b1 also deserves consideration.

| 15 | ... | | ♕b6 | 73 |
| 16 | ♗b1 | 82 | | |

Kasparov spent 35 minutes on this. Also possible is the manoeuvre ♘e2-f4.

16	...		♗b7	85
17	♕c2	86	g6	85
18	d5	88		

| 18 | ... | | ed | 95 |

The tempting 18 ... ♗xc3 would have been answered with 19 ♖xe6 fe 20 ♕xg6+ ♗g7 21 ♕h7+ ♔f7 22 de+ ♕xe6 23 ♖xd7+ ♕xd7 24 ♘e5+ and White wins.

19	♘xd5	89	♗xd5	95
20	♖xd5	89	♖fd8	99
	Draw Agreed			

Karpov appeared to offer the draw, which was accepted after some minutes' thought. Handshake. No post mortem. Karpov looked content. An ominous sign that Kasparov could derive no advantage at all from the opening.

| Karpov | 0 | ½ | ½ | 1 |
| Kasparov | 1 | ½ | ½ | 2 |

GAME FOUR, 12-13 September

Karpov's first win against Kasparov for 24 games! It was, in fact, a jewel of finesse and precision which must rank amongst the World Champion's greatest masterpieces. It was, for example, in the same mould as Karpov's victory in the 9th game of their former contest, his first round win against Ulf Andersson in the USSR-World match, London 1984, and his classic demolition of Korchnoi in the GLC tournament, also in London earlier that year.

The applause for Kasparov at the start of the game was twice as loud and long as for Karpov. As usual, Kasparov arrived at the board first. The opening moves came carefully from both players, with Karpov following his triumphant fifth win from game 27 of the first match. The variation chosen developed along interesting lines with Kasparov's 8th move, ... ♘a6, constituting a novelty. White soon fixed Black's d-pawn (IQP) as a potential weakness, but Kasparov held the bishop pair and control of the c-file as compensation.

Thereafter, Karpov formed the plan of exchanging a knight for Black's queen's bishop and then attempting to attack via the light squares against Black's central pawns and ultimately his king.

At adjournment, when Karpov sealed his 41st move, Kasparov's pawns were scattered and his king exposed to attack from White's queen and bishop along the b1-h7 diagonal. Furthermore, White had the possibility of advancing his kingside pawns to augment his offensive. In the second session of play, Karpov also succeeded in introducing his apparently dormant rook into the attack by virtue of some wonderfully subtle manoeuvres. After White's 63rd move, creating a model of centralisation, Karpov's pieces dominated the entire board and Black could not avoid mate or ruinous losses of material.

A marvellous game by the Champion, marked by a deep and restrained strategy which culminated in an overwhelming onslaught. As Tony Miles has said, Karpov has a very fine feeling for probing sensitive points, and this was very much in evidence in game 4.

Karpov-Kasparov
Queen's Gambit Declined

1	d4	0	d5	2
2	c4	3	e6	2
3	♘c3	6	♗e7	6
4	♘f3	13	♘f6	6
5	♗g5	13	h6	6
6	♗xf6	14	♗xf6	6
7	e3	15	0-0	6
8	♕c2	15		

Now 8 ... c5 9 dc ♕a5 10 cd ed 11 0-0-0 ♗e6 12 ♘xd5 is Kasparov-Timman, USSR-World 1984, a classic win by Kasparov.

Alternatively, 8 ... c5 9 dc dc 10 ♗xc4 ♕a5 11 0-0 ♗xc3 12 ♕xc3 ♕xc3 13 bc. This was Karpov-Kasparov, match 1984-85 (27), the last occasion on which Karpov had beaten Kasparov.

| 8 | ... | | ♘a6!? | 15 |

This came as a shock, a completely new move. Interestingly, Kasparov thought for nine minutes before playing it, and Karpov returned the compliment with interest by spending 24 minutes on his reply.

| 9 | ♖d1 | 39 | | |

Other moves worthy of consideration are 9 cd ♘b4 10 ♕b3 ♘xd5 11 ♖c1, or 9 c5 b6 10 ♕a4 ♘b8 and now either 11 c6 or 11 b4. But faced with an innovation it is usually best to avoid adventures. Karpov's move is solid and good.

| 9 | ... | | c5 | 18 |
| 10 | dc | 51 | | |

Perhaps 10 cd ♕a5 11 de ♗xe6 12 d5 ♘b4. This would, however, not be consistent with his policy of avoiding adventure.

| 10 | ... | | ♕a5 | 23 |
| 11 | cd | 51 | ♘xc5 | 23 |

Both players played their 11th move immediately and Karpov continued quckly and confidently with the positional plan which he had conceived. For example, 12 d6? would be dangerous after 12 ... ♖d8, while 12 de ♗xc3+ 13 ♕xc3 ♕xc3+ 14 bc ♗xe6 15 c4 ♖fc8 16 ♗e2 ♘e4 is comfortable for Black. Also interesting, but less clear, is 12 de ♗xe6 13 ♘d4.

| 12 | ♕d2 | 60 | ♖d8 | 35 |
| 13 | ♘d4! | 63 | | |

White renounces any thought of trying to snatch material and plays instead for the solid advantage of a blockade against Black's isolated queen's pawn.

| 13 | ... | | ed | 43 |

In the press room Chiburdanidze was already predicting moves 14-17 well before they were played.

14	♗e2	*63*	♕b6	*50*
15	0-0	*63*	♘e4	*51*

Another approach is 15 ... ♘e6, though White retains some edge with 16 ♗f3.

16	♕c2	*67*	♘xc3	*58*
17	♕xc3	*68*	♗e6	*60*

In the press centre Dorfman advocated 17 ... ♗f5, e.g. 18 ♕b3 ♕xb3 19 ab ♗e4 20 ♖dc1 ♖d6 and ... ♖b6. But Kasparov walked around the stage confidently after 17 ... ♗e6.

18	♕c2	*83*	♖ac8	*65*
19	♕b1	*83*		

An unusual post for the queen, but time is not of the essence here and there is plenty of scope for the queen to re-emerge.

19	...		♖c7	*78*
20	♖d2	*86*	♖dc8?!	*89*

This was, perhaps, a mistake. Passive though it is, 20 ... ♗xd4 might have given superior drawing chances.

21	♘xe6	*88*	fe	*90*

21 ... ♕xe6 would run the risk of losing the IQP. The text, however, leaves Black with a permanent wound along the b1-h7 diagonal. The full effects of this will be seen if White can ever line up his queen and bishop along it. Black cannot, of course, construct a pawn barricade against long-term evil by playing ... g6 (as Karpov had done in game 3) since he has already committed himself to ... h6. The other problem Black now faces is that his pawn duo on d5 and e6 becomes strikingly wooden and inflexible. On top of this, if White can arrange to punch Black's central pawn constellation with a well-timed e4 thrust, there is a danger that further weaknesses will be opened up behind Black's lines, for example, on the e6 square.

Having said this, Black's position must still be defensible, since the opposite bishops also represent a potent force for defence as well as operating in White's favour as a weapon of aggression.

22	♗g4	*89*	

Karpov glanced up at Kasparov after playing this move and looked pleased.

22	...		♖c4	*101*
23	h3	*91*	♕c6	*103*
24	♕d3	*96*	♔h8	*108*

Kasparov was strolling around at this point but this was, perhaps, a psychological ploy (generating confident body language) to counter Karpov, who was evidently satisfied with his ♕d3 and was now playing contentedly with his hair.

| 25 | ♖fd1 | *102* | a5 | *109* |
| 26 | b3 | *105* | ♖c3 | *115* |

This represents a small victory for Black, who now has an outpost for his rook.

27 ♕e2 *106*

If 27 ♕g6 then 27 ... ♕e8!. Naturally, White must absolutely avoid the exchange of queens.

| 27 | ... | | ♖f8 | *116* |
| 28 | ♗h5! | *117* | | |

An excellent concept, intending to transfer the bishop to the critical b1-h7 diagonal.

28 ... b5?! *120*

He might have profited from the temporary respite to play the immediate 28 ... ♗d8, intending ... ♗b6.

29 ♗g6 *117*

Played instantly. Each player had half an hour left for the last eleven moves.

29	...		♗d8	*123*
30	♗d3	*123*	b4	*124*
31	♕g4	*123*	♕e8	*127*
32	e4!	*128*		

The thematic central blow, placing maximum stress on Black's structure. If Black plays 32 ... d4 then 33 e5 ♗g5 34 ♖c2 ♖f4 35 ♕e2.

32 ... ♗g5 *136*

The point of this is to force an exchange of rooks. Nevertheless, it might be better to strike at f2 with ... ♗b6.

33 ♖c2 *128*

Not 33 ♖e2?? ♖f4 34 ♕g3 de and Black wins.

33 ... ♖xc2 *143*

This move has come in for a lot of criticism since it seems ridiculous to abandon the hard-won outpost at c3, but if 33 ... ♕c6 White can simply play 34 ed ed 35 ♖e2! escaping the exchange and seizing the e-file. By trading rooks, Kasparov gains time to regroup his defences. Black even appears to create a slight initiative, though the long-term positional defects of his position will not run away.

34	♗xc2	*128*	♕c6	*144*
35	♕e2	*133*	♕c5	*144*
36	♖f1	*133*		

A mysterious rook move. But Black had been threatening ... ♖xf2 and ... ♗e3. White's rook stays glued to f1 for some time to come, but when Karpov does eventually free it, it plays a decisive role.

36	...		♕c3	145
37	ed	138	ed	145
38	♗b1	143	♕d2	145
39	♕e5!	149		

With this move White's queen achieves the freedom to attack. The move also prevents ... ♗h4, which can now be met with g3 and it is, of course, much stronger than the penny-pinching 39 ♕xd2 ♗xd2 40 ♖d1.

| 39 | ... | | ♖d8? | 148 |

This may be the decisive error by Kasparov. After 39 ... ♗f6 to be followed by ... ♗d4 his position might still be tenable.

| 40 | ♕f5 | 149 | ♔g8 | 149 |

Karpov sealed his 41st move. White's plan must be to tidy up his position with g3, h4 and ♔g2. His next task will be to find a way of introducing his rook into the attack. White's queen and bishop, dangerous though they are, cannot win on their own.

Although opinions were divided at adjournment on whether Karpov was winning, overnight analysis convinced experts that the position was very bad for Kasparov and almost certainly lost.

41	♕e6+	156	♔h8	149
42	♕g6	156	♔g8	149
43	♕e6+	156	♔h8	149
44	♗f5	156	♕c3	149
45	♕g6	156	♔g8	149
46	♗e6+	159	♔h8	149
47	♗f5	159	♔g8	149
48	g3	165	♔f8	153
49	♔g2	170	♕f6	162
50	♕h7	172	♕f7	162
51	h4	173	♗d2?	164

A more obstinate defence arises from 51 ... ♗f6 52 ♖e1 ♕g8 53 ♕g6 ♕f7 54 ♕g4 h5 55 ♕f4 d4, though after 56 ♗d3 it still looks grim.

| 52 | ♖d1 | 174 | ♗c3 | 164 |
| 53 | ♖d3 | 183 | ♖d6 | 181 |

Dorfman admitted at move 53 that the position was losing.

| 54 | ♖f3 | 185 | ♔e7 | 189 |
| 55 | ♕h8! | 206 | | |

If 55 ♖e3+ ♔d8 56 ♕h8+ ♔c7 and Black might escape. 55 ♕h8 finishes the game.

| 55 | ... | | d4 | 201 |
| 56 | ♕c8 | 209 | ♖f6 | 207 |

While Karpov was thinking about his 57th move, the youngest arbiter, the Lithuanian Lembit

Vachessar, brought him a cup of coffee, or maybe tea, but dropped the saucer. The resultant clatter broke the usually subdued and restrained silence in the room. But Lembit recovered well and replaced the saucer under the cup.

57	♕c5+	225	♔e8	210
58	♖f4	230	♕b7+	212
59	♖e4+	230	♔f7	215

If 59 ... ♖e6 60 ♕c4 and ♕g8+.

60	♕c4+	242	♔f8	215
61	♗h7	242	♖f7	217
62	♕e6	245	♕d7	217
63	♕e5	245		

Black resigns

63 ... ♕d8 64 ♕c5+ ♖e7 65 ♖f4+ ♔e8 66 ♕c6+ ♕d7 67 ♗g6+, or 63 ... ♖e7 64 ♕f4+ ♖f7 65 ♕b8+.

"Karpov is capable of transforming the most minute advantage into a crushing position and he weaves a fine mesh of moves with the relentless care of a spider building a web." – Dominic Lawson, *Financial Times*

Grandmaster Eddie Gufeld summed up: "It was a game of big manoeuvres, but in these manoeuvres Karpov played better. His genius lies with this kind of strategic technique."

Kasparov's failure to take a time-out after game 4 was an obvious mistake. It reminds one of his omission in the last match to take a time-out after game 6. He then went straight on to lose game 7. Still, a fine win for Karpov and now the onus has to be on Kasparov to do something.

Karpov	0	½	½	1	2
Kasparov	1	½	½	0	2

GAME FIVE, 14 September

In contrast to the super form the Champion is now finding, Kasparov appears to have abruptly cracked up and is ominously losing the kind of game which cost him so many points during the disastrous first nine of the previous match. As Black he was saddled with a weak isolated queen's pawn in game 4, highly reminiscent of games 7 and 9 from 1984. In game 5 he gave up a pawn for nebulous attacking chances and eventually succumbed to an extra black pawn on the queenside, which was sadly redolent of game 6 from last year. We wonder whether Kasparov has not fallen prey to his old disease of over-confidence.

At the start of the game there was equal applause for both players, Kasparov appearing first as usual. Klara, his mother, sat in her customary seat in the fourth row on the far left. When Kasparov was doing badly in the last match she moved to the press balcony at the back and watched through opera glasses. Will she do the same now? The first ten or twenty moves came quickly from both players, but Kasparov looked up at Karpov after 2 ♘f3. Karpov conceded no counterplay once the pawn was lost. Kasparov screwed his elbows to the table, sat rigid almost like a statue, but with his right leg shaking from time to time, searching for counterplay. Karpov walked round a little but used all his remaining time to avoid complications. On adjournment Kasparov resigned without resuming.

Kasparov-Karpov					5	0-0	2	♗e7	1
Ruy Lopez					6	♖e1	2	b5	1
					7	♗b3	2	d6	3
1	e4	1	e5	0	8	c3	2	0-0	3
2	♘f3	1	♘c6	1	9	h3	2	♗b7	8
3	♗b5	1	a6	1	10	d4	2	♖e8	8
4	♗a4	1	♘f6	1	11	♘bd2	3	♗f8	16

70

12 a4 7

If 12 d5 ♘e7! with ideas of sacrificing a knight for White's central pawns, either on e4 or d5. Geller-Eingorn, 52nd USSR Ch, Riga 1985, exemplified this concept: 12 d5 ♘e7 13 ♗c2 g6 14 ♘f1 ♗g7 15 b3 ♘xe4!? 16 ♗xe4 f5 17 ♗c2 e4 18 ♘d4 ♘xd5 and here Geller abandoned another pawn with 19 ♘e2 ♘xc3 and went on to lose. 19 ♗d2!? has been advocated as a possible improvement.

12	...		♛d7	23
13	ab	23	ab	23
14	♖xa8	24	♗xa8	23
15	d5	25		

15 ... ♘a5 28

Karpov had spent only six minutes on 12 ... ♛d7, and 15 ... ♘a5 was obviously prepared and an improvement over his 15 ... ♘d8 from game 46 last time. It is worth quoting the interesting continuation of game 46: 15 d5 ♘d8 16 ♘f1 h6 17 ♘3h2 ♘b7 (playing the knight away from a square

which turns out to be extremely useful in the present game) 18 ♗c2 ♘c5 19 b4 ♘a6 20 ♘g4 ♘h7 21 ♘g3 c6 22 dc ♗xc6 23 ♗b3 ♘c7 24 ♛f3 ♘e6 25 h4 ♛d8 26 ♖d1 ♛a8 and here Kasparov played 27 ♗d5?, overlooking the brilliant, if recondite, win with 27 ♗xh6! gh 28 ♖xd6!! ♗xd6 29 ♘xh6+ leading to a crushing attack. In this fresh encounter Karpov resolves to play less passively. In particular he wastes less time with his queen's knight and strives for a more rapid break with ... c6.

16	♗a2	29	c6	31
17	b4	29	♘b7	31
18	c4	31		

18 ♘f1 cd 19 ed ±, or 18 ... h6 19 ♘3h2 ♘d8 20 ♘g4 ±.

18 ... ♖c8! 51

A deep and excellent move, looking forward to a future exploitation of weaknesses in White's queenside pawn structure. If instead the plausible 18 ... c5, then 19 ♗a3! with a clear advantage.

19 dc 43

19 ♗b2 ♘d8 20 ♛a1 ♖b8 21 dc ♗xc6 22 ♖d1 ±.

19	...		♛xc6	51
20	c5?	43		

The press room grandmasters criticised 20 c5 as giving up the central tension too early. Better perhaps 20 ♛e2!?. Anyway, 20 c5 was played immediately. It looks enticing to blast open the a2-g8

71

B

W

24 ...   ♕b4   88

diagonal and simultaneously undermine Black's e5 pawn by striking
at the d6 base, but White is not yet
sufficiently well developed to profit
from such activity. Black's next
very fine prophylactic retreat the-
matically protects f7 and draws
the sting from White's attack.

20 ...   ♘d8!   67
21 ♗b2   47   dc   84
22 bc   47

Not good. It was better to capture on e5, though 22 ♘xe5 ♕a6
23 ♗b1 c4 24 ♗c3 ♕a3 is hardly
inviting for White. Suddenly it
looked worse for Kasparov and
the GMs in the press room spent a
long time looking at ways to stop
Karpov's pieces reactivating.

22 ...   ♕xc5   84
23 ♗xe5   50   ♘d7   87
24 ♗b2   65

He should prefer 24 ♗a1. Black's
c-file control and passed pawn are
already far more significant than
any kingside attacking chances
White may have.

25 ♘b3?   95
The key position. Kasparov
spent half an hour on 25 ♘b3.
25 ♕b1 or 25 ♕a1 would be better.
It is time to abandon all thoughts
of aggression.

25 ...   ♘c5!   95
"Simply and convincingly White's
position quickly deteriorates. He
cannot, of course, play 26 ♘xc5?
because of 26 ... ♕xb2, and on 26
♕c1 possible is 26 ... ♗b7 or 26 ...
♕a4. Kasparov prefers to part
with a pawn." (Suetin)

26 ♗a1   105
The press room was amazed by
this move, played after less than
ten minutes' thought. 26 ♘fd4
♘d3 27 ♖e2 ♘xb2 and 26 e5 ♗xf3
27 gf ♘d3! are both horrible. In
spite of what Suetin says, perhaps
26 ♘xc5 ♕xb2 27 ♕b3 ♕xb3 28
♘xb3 is the best chance.

26 ...   ♗xe4   105
27 ♘fd4   117
If 27 ♘g5 ♗c2!.

27	...		♘db7	109
28	♕e2	128	♘d6	112
29	♘xc5	129	♕xc5	114
30	♕g4	132	♖e8	115
31	♖d1	134	♗g6	117
32	♕f4	136	♕b4	124
33	♕c1	137	♗e4	136
34	♖e1	138	♕a5	139
35	♗b3	139	♕a8	140
36	♕b2	141		

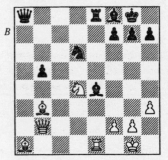

| 36 | ... | | b4 | 142 |

"Black's chief trump card, the

b-pawn, moves forward. Besides, Black establishes control over the c3 square. But what is the reason why Black does not take the g2 pawn either now or on the next move? If he does, e.g. (after 37 ♖e3) 37 ... ♗xg2, possible is 38 ♖xe8 ♘xe8 39 ♘f5 threatening the unpleasant ♘h6+. If Black answers 39 ♘f5 by 39 ... ♕c6 then White would be able to continue 40 ♗a4, and on 40 ... ♕g6 possible is 41 ♘h4. Karpov prefers a calm way of cashing in on his edge." (Suetin)

37	♖e3	144	♗g6	144
38	♖xe8	145	♕xe8	144
39	♕c1	145	♘e4	145
40	♗d5	146	♘c5	146
41	♘b3	148	♘d3	152

The sealed move, and **Kasparov resigned** without resumption.

After game 5, with the score at

| Karpov | 0 ½ ½ 1 1 | 3 |
| Kasparov | 1 ½ ½ 0 0 | 2 |

Kasparov took his first time out.

In interviews with Defence Ministry Newspaper *Krasnaya Zvezda* (Red Star) and mass circulation *Sovietskaya Rossiya* (Soviet Russia), Karpov said he had underestimated the need for psychological preparation before the last match. "Recently I increased attention to psychological preparation." He criticised the FIDE two-year-cycle ruling, saying it was aimed at "preventing a world champion from sitting on the chess throne for a long time . . . This will result in a rapid change of chess generations and will hardly benefit chess".

GAME SIX, 19 September

An important game for Kasparov, who had set out to restore his equilibrium after his two losses. His pawn sacrifice gave his supporters some uneasy moments, but in the end he held fairly easily with Black and the match is anything but over. Although GMs had at first felt Karpov stood better, opinions changed after he won the pawn. At move 22 Dorfman said "Nichya" (draw), while at move 23 Gufeld said it seemed enough for a draw. We asked Yusupov if White had any winning chances and he said he wasn't sure, but if there were any they were based on pushing the queenside pawns, which Karpov decided not to risk.

Karpov-Kasparov
Queen's Gambit Declined

1	d4	*1*	d5	*0*
2	c4	*1*	e6	*0*
3	♘c3	*3*	♗e7	*0*
4	♘f3	*4*	♘f6	*0*
5	♗g5	*4*	h6	*0*
6	♗xf6	*4*	♗xf6	*0*
7	e3	*5*	0-0	*0*
8	♕d2	*5*	dc	*8*
9	♗xc4	*5*	♘d7	*9*
10	0-0	*9*	c5	*10*
11	♖fd1	*9*	cd	*14*
12	♘xd4	*10*	♘b6	*18*
13	♗e2!	*10*		

The game Belyavsky-Portisch, Tilburg 1984, went 13 ♗b3 ♗d7 14 ♘e4 ♗xd4 15 ♕xd4 ♗c6 16 ♘d6? ♕e7 17 e4 ♖ad8 18 ♕e5

♖d7 19 ♖d3 ♕f6 20 ♕xf6 gf and Black was better.

13 ♗e2, intending to hit the queenside with ♗f3, is an improvement.

13	...		♗d7	*26*
14	♗f3	*16*	♖b8	*30*
15	♘e4	*26*	♗xd4	*37*

If 15 ... ♗e7, 16 ♖ac1 leaves White better, but Kasparov must have planned the pawn sacrifice already.

| 16 | ♕xd4 | *26* | ♗a4 | *42* |

Not 16 ... ♗c6 17 ♕c5 ♕c7 18 ♘d6.

| 17 | ♕xd8 | *33* | | |

After 17 b3 then 17 ... ♕xd4 18 ♖xd4 ♗c6 is not very much for White.

| 17 | ... | | ♖fxd8 | *43* |

74

18	♖xd8+	34	♖xd8	43
19	♘c5	34	♖d2	45
20	b3	38	♗c6	45
21	♘xb7	38	♗xf3	45
22	gf	38	♘d7	47

Black now has compensation with his active rook and play against the weakened kingside pawns.

23	♔g2	65

If 23 f4 then Taimanov suggested 23 ... g5. Also possible is 23 ... ♘f6 intending ... ♘g4.

23	...		g5	50

A mistake would be 23 ... ♘e5?. Yuri Kotkov, writing in *Sovietsky Sport*, gives 24 ♘c5 ♖c2 25 b4 ♘c4 26 ♔g3 ♘a3 27 ♖d1 a5 28 ♖d8+ ♔h7 29 ♘d7 ab 30 ♘f8+ ♔g8 31 ♘xe6+ ♔h7 32 ♘f8+ ♔g8 33 ♖b8 ♖xa2 34 ♘d7+ ♔h7 35 ♖xb4, and White must have good winning chances.

24	b4	75	♘b6	68

This threatens a fork at d5. In the press centre we were looking at 24 ... ♘e5 25 ♘c5 ♘c4 26 ♔g3 ♘a3 27 ♘b3 ♖b2, trying to tie White in knots.

25	♔f1	81

If 25 a4 ♘d5 26 b5 ♘xe3+ 27 ♔g1 ♘c2 28 ♖b1 ♘d4.

25 ♔g3 is dangerous because of 25 ... h5.

25	...		♘d7	69

26	♔g2	107

The most active try is 26 a4, e.g. 26 ... ♘e5 27 b5 ♘d3 28 a5 ♖xf2+ 29 ♔g1 ♖d2 30 f4 (30 b6 ♘e5) 30 ... gf 31 ef ♘xf4 32 b6 ab 33 a6 ♘d5 34 a7 ♘c7 35 ♖c1 ♖a2 =. If 27 ... ♘xf3 28 a5 ♘xh2+ 29 ♔g1 (29 ♔g2 ♘g4 30 b6 ab 31 a6 ♘xe3+ 32 ♔g3 ♘d5 33 a7 ♘c7 34 ♖c1 ♖a2 35 ♖xc7 ♖xa7) 29 ... ♘f3+ 30 ♔g2 ♘e5 31 b6 ab 32 a6 ♘c6 33 a7 ♘xa7 34 ♖xa7 ♖d7 35 ♖a8+ ♔g7 36 ♖b8. It is hard to believe that Black could lose this.

26	...		♘b6	87
27	♔f1	117	♘d7	87

After 27 minutes Karpov reconciled himself to a draw. If 28 ♘c5 then 28 ... ♘e5 29 b5 ♘d3 30 ♘b3 ♖xf2+ 31 ♔g1 ♖b2, or 28 a3 ♘e5 29 ♖c1 ♘xf3 30 ♔g2 g4, when ... h5 and ... ♖a2 are coming. It's interesting how long Karpov spent on moves 23 to the end.

Draw Agreed

Karpov	0	½	½	1	1	½	3½
Kasparov	1	½	½	0	0	½	2½

GAME SEVEN, 21 September

Kasparov bounced back into action in a rich, wild and difficult game that had GMs in the press centre unable to predict not only the moves but also who stood better. As usual Kasparov arrived early, but Karpov sat for four minutes before playing 1 ... ♘f6, obviously some sort of psychological warfare. Early in the game Klara Kasparova was briefly seen studying the players and arbiters on the stage through opera glasses – in spite of the fact that she was sitting in the third row.

The general opinion was that White stood better from the opening and GMs criticised Karpov's 17 ... ♔f7. But after Kasparov's 23rd move assessments changed to 'better for Black', and when Karpov pondered seven minutes over his obvious 26th move observers were prompted to speculate that Kasparov had offered a draw.

Before playing 26 ♘e5+ Kasparov began to look worried for the first time in the game, but Karpov was left with only five minutes for the last thirteen moves and allowed Kasparov to force a draw by perpetual check after 31 ♖xd5! ed 32 ♕f5+ etc.

Kasparov-Karpov
Nimzo-Indian Defence

Notes marked 'T' are by Taimanov

1	d4	1	♘f6	4
2	c4	1	e6	4
3	♘c3	1	♗b4	4
4	♘f3	1	0-0	9
5	♗g5	4	d6	11
6	e3	13	♘bd7	13
7	♕c2	31		

Black's counterplay is based on undermining White's pawn centre by advancing ... e5. (T)

7	...		b6	14
8	♗d3	32	♗xc3+	18
9	bc	38	h6	38
10	♗h4	38	♗b7	41
11	♘d2	41	g5	67

An unexpected and very bold decision. In his bid to counterattack, the World Champion consciously

76

goes for a sharp weakening of his king's position. (T)

Less satisfactory continuations are 11 ... ♗xg2 12 ♖g1 ♗b7 13 0-0-0 and 11 ... e5 12 0-0 ♕e7 13 f3.

12	♗g3	*41*	♘h5	*67*
13	♕d1!?	*63*		

More natural would be 13 f3 ♘xg3 14 hg ♔g7 15 g4 trying to play his knight to g3 via f1. Or perhaps even 13 f4!?.

13	...		♘g7	*69*
14	h4	*66*	f5	*72*

Black succeeds in blocking the approaches to his king. (T)

15	hg	*66*	hg	*72*
16	f3	*67*	♕e7	*80*
17	♕b3	*69*	♔f7	*85*

An unexpected move by Karpov. By playing 17 ... c5 18 0-0-0 ♘f6 the World Champion would have obtained a stable and promising position. (T)

18	0-0-0	*70*	♖h8	*86*

The blockading move 18 ... c5 looked attractive. But now White again succeeds in seizing the initiative. (T)

19	c5!	*71*		

By sacrificing a pawn Kasparov revitalises his distant bishops and stresses the vulnerability of Black's king. (T)

19	...	.	dc	*91*
20	♘c4	*73*	cd	*104*
21	cd	*75*	f4!?	*123*

Very risky, since White could now have played 22 ef ♘h5 23

♖xh5 ♖xh5 24 f5 ♗d5 25 ♖e1 ♖h6 26 ♗e4 ♗xe4 27 ♖xe4 with a dangerous initiative for the sacrificed exchange. The press centre had been expecting a less belligerent defence, namely 21 ... ♖xh1 22 ♖xh1 ♗d5 23 e4 ♗xc4 24 ♗xc4 b5, or perhaps 23 ♕b2!?.

22	♗f2	*85*	♘h5	*127*
23	♗c2?!	*107*		

Allowing the initiative to fade. Why not 23 e4 threatening d5? That way White would keep his central pawns mobile. Also 23 ♖he1 is worth considering.

23	...		fe	*134*
24	♗xe3	*109*	♗d5	*134*
25	♕d3	*111*	♖ag8	*135*
26	♘e5+	*121*		

Or 26 g4 ♘f4 27 ♗xf4 gf 28 ♖h7+ ♖xh7 29 ♕xh7+ ♔f8 30 ♕h6+ ♔e8 and White runs out of steam.

26	...		♘xe5	*143*
27	de	*121*	♘f4	*143*

Karpov was now in severe time trouble. At first everyone believed that he might have played for a win with 27 ... c6 to solidify the bishop on d5, but then comes 28 罝h2 (as suggested by Jon Tisdall) 28 ... ♘f4 29 ♗xf4 gf 30 罝dh1 罝xh2 31 罝xh2 罝g7 32 罝h6 with numerous threats such as 罝f6+ and 曾a6. Maybe better, though, is 27 ... c5! intending ... ♘g3 or ... ♘f4 and ... c4 to rule out 曾a6.

White now seizes the opportunity to force a draw – necessary since his own king is also quite exposed.

28	♗xf4	127	gf	143
29	罝xh8	128	罝xh8	143
30	曾g6+	128	♔f8	144
31	罝xd5!	128	Draw Agreed	

The game ends in an unexpected draw. Black could find no escape from perpetual check. (T)

Karpov	0 ½ ½ 1 1 ½ ½	4
Kasparov	1 ½ ½ 0 0 ½ ½	3

On Monday 23 September the experienced Yugoslav reporter-photographer Ratko Knežević who works for Tanjug, the Yugoslav news agency, left town. Knežević, who has reported on five Olympiads and the last three title contests, was consistently refused accreditation to cover the match, even though his visa enables him to come to Moscow regularly. The official reason was that too many (six) Yugoslavs were already accredited. Knežević claimed his non-accreditation was due to a *Spiegel*-style interview he did with Kasparov in the 9 June edition of the Belgrade newspaper *Sport* entitled "Never Trust Campomanes". Ratko was not accredited despite a supporting letter from Tanjug chess editor and FIDE Executive Council member Božidar Kažić which quoted a FIDE regulation: "Every journalist shall receive a pass". In view of the title of the article, it was a strange decision on the part of Kažić to address this letter to Campomanes himself. When asked, Campomanes said: "Every state has a right to handle its own internal affairs . . . I passed the letter to the appropriate authorities". This story even made it into the official Yugoslav Communist Party newspaper *Politika*.

GAME EIGHT, 24-25 September

Play in this game was reminiscent of a number of Queen's Gambits from the earlier marathon. Although Karpov held a nominal advantage throughout and even had an extra pawn at adjournment, he never came within realistic sight of scoring a win. He continued his policy of pondering early moves by sitting for thirteen minutes before playing 4 ♘f3. Was he considering an Exchange Variation? More probably he was, in some obscure way, extending his earlier psychological tactics.

The atmosphere was restrained today in the hall and the press room, but Karpov looked confident and Polugayevsky and Gufeld were predicting that he would try to squeeze out a win. He played moves 24-32 quickly, as he often does when having a clear technical advantage.

Polugayevsky commented that the adjourned position was a well known theoretical draw. Karpov's desire to play on can only be explained, again, by purely psychological reasons.

	Karpov-Kasparov				
	Queen's Gambit Declined		12	bc	27	bc	16

Karpov-Kasparov
Queen's Gambit Declined

	White		Black	
1	d4	2	d5	0
2	c4	2	e6	0
3	♘c3	3	♗e7	1
4	♘f3	16	♘f6	1
5	♗g5	20	h6	7
6	♗h4	21	0-0	7
7	e3	21	b6	10
8	♗e2	26	♗b7	10
9	♗xf6	27	♗xf6	10
10	cd	27	ed	10
11	b4	27	c5	16
12	bc	27	bc	16
13	♖b1	27	♗c6	16
14	0-0	28	♘d7	17
15	♗b5	28	♕c7	17

79

16 ♕d3   *40*

In the 12th game of the previous match Kasparov, as White, had played 16 ♕d2, while 16 ♕c2 was tested in three other games – 38, 39 and 42. 16 ♕d3 had already been seen in the game Vladimirov-Didishko, Spartakiad 1983: 16 ... ♖fd8 17 ♕f5 cd 18 ed g6 19 ♕h3 ♗xb5 20 ♘xb5 ♕f4. It is clear that when analysing this game the World Champion found a way to improve White's play.

16	...		♖fd8	*24*
17	♖fd1	*57*	♖ab8	*42*
18	♗xc6	*66*	♕xc6	*56*
19	♖xb8	*66*	♖xb8	*61*
20	dc	*67*	♗xc3	*62*
21	♕xc3	*68*	♕xc5	*62*
22	♕xc5	*75*	♘xc5	*62*
23	h3	*75*		

"The chessboard now looks as if a storm has hit it. White has a better pawn configuration but Black still has scope for action." (Taimanov)

23	...		♘e4	*87*

"A device characteristic of Kasparov, reminiscent of his plans in the sixth game. Unwilling to defend himself passively by the move 23 ... ♖d8, he immediately parts with a pawn, counting on active counterplay." (Taimanov)

24	♖xd5	*75*	♖b1+	*92*
25	♔h2	*75*	♘xf2	*96*
26	♖d8+	*75*	♔h7	*96*
27	♖d7	*75*	a5	*102*
28	♖xf7	*76*	♖b2	*102*
29	h4	*84*	♘d1	*106*

"Kasparov's calculation turns out to be correct. The number of combat forces on the board diminishes and White's extra pawn loses its importance." (Taimanov)

30	♖e7	*85*	♖b4	*112*
31	♘d4	*94*	♘xe3	*113*

31 ... ♖xa4 was also a possibility and if 32 ♘f5 then 32 ... ♔g6.

32	♘c6	*95*	♖c4	*114*
33	♖xe3	*95*	♖xc6	*114*
34	♖e5	*95*	♖c3	*114*

Rather than assume the defensive by 34 ... ♖a6 Kasparov again sacrifices to activate his rook.

35	♖xa5	*95*	♖a3	*114*
36	h4	*97*	♔g6	*125*
37	g4	*109*	♔f6	*137*
38	♖f5+	*117*	♔e6	*137*
39	♖f4	*117*	g5	*141*
40	hg	*117*	hg	*141*
41	♖b4	*117*	♔e5	*183*

The sealed move.

42	♔g2	*118*	♖a2+	*184*
43	♔f3	*119*	♖a3+	*184*
44	♔e2	*119*	♖g3	*184*
45	♔d2	*119*	♖g2+	*185*
46	♔e3	*125*	♖g3+	*185*
47	♔e2	*125*	♖a3	*186*
48	♔d2	*128*	♖g3	*186*
49	♖c4	*128*	♔d5	*186*

Draw Agreed

Karpov	0	½	½	1	1	½	½	½	4½
Kasparov	1	½	½	0	0	½	½	½	3½

GAME NINE, 26-27 September

In spite of the sequence of draws, the games have been bitterly fought, especially game 9. In a world championship match the feeling in the playing hall is predominantly one of great tension. In contrast, the "live action" goes on in the press room, where rival groups of grandmasters try to outshine each other in impromptu ingenious analysis.

In the opening the two continued their Ruy Lopez dispute from game 5. The regular analysis team at the match – Taimanov, Averbakh, Gufeld, Polugayevsky – were joined by Timoshchenko (Kasparov camp) for the first half of the session and by Vasyukov (Karpov camp) for the second half. Kasparov's 19 b3 indicated he wanted to start a war of attrition with slow and quiet manoeuvring. Polugayevsky and Vasyukov tried to show that Black was equal during the quiet stage, but eventually had to concede that White stood better. The grandmaster room was packed out. Karpov defended well and at adjournment, after Kasparov had over-reached, many thought Karpov might even win.

In the second session the first moves came fast, but after the superhuman move 45 e5! Karpov sank deep into thought for 34 minutes. In the press room Dorfman and Timoshchenko appeared cool and unbothered, but were obviously pleased to have out-analysed the Karpov camp. One other idea is 45 ♕b5 ♗c6 46 ♕a5 ♘b7 47 ♕b6 ♕c5: unclear. When we asked Dorfman what would happen after 45 e5 he just smiled and said "Wait and see". It also bowled over the GMs in the press centre, but they were eventually able to predict the final position on their boards before it was reached on the stage. Kasparov spent only three minutes on the whole of the second session and used almost the same amount of time at the board, preferring to walk around or go backstage. He only remained seated after 53 ♔g2, obviously expecting a draw, and after a few minutes the hands came up simultaneously.

81

Kasparov-Karpov
Ruy Lopez

1	e4	*2*	e5	*0*
2	♘f3	*2*	♘c6	*0*
3	♗b5	*2*	a6	*0*
4	♗a4	*2*	♘f6	*0*
5	0-0	*2*	♗e7	*0*
6	♖e1	*2*	b5	*0*
7	♗b3	*2*	d6	*5*
8	c3	*2*	0-0	*5*
9	h3	*2*	♗b7	*7*
10	d4	*2*	♖e8	*7*
11	♘bd2	*2*	♗f8	*9*
12	a4	*2*	h6	*11*

12 ... ♕d7 would have transposed back into game 5, but Karpov obviously feared an improvement.

13	♗c2	*2*	

13 d5 ♘b8 14 c4 c6 15 ab ab 16 ♖xa8 ♗xa8 17 dc was a Kasparov-Dorfman game from a previous Soviet Championship, but Black was OK, so Kasparov deploys his bishop at d3 to pressure b5.

13	...		♘b8	*11*
14	♗d3	*5*	c6	*11*
15	♘f1	*19*		

Also good is 15 b4 and ♘b3.

15	...		♘bd7	*14*
16	♘g3	*19*	♕c7	*25*
17	♗d2	*26*	g6	*46*

The grandmasters looked at 17 ... d5, but 18 ed ♘xd5 19 ab ab 20 ♖xa8 ♗xa8 21 ♗f5 seems good.

18	♕c1	*37*	♔h7	*49*
19	b3	*56*		

More aggressive is 19 h4! ♗g7

20 h5, threatening ♘h4 and f4.

19	...		♗g7	*52*
20	♕c2	*63*	♘f8	*73*
21	♗e3	*87*	♘e6	*74*
22	♖ad1	*93*	♖ac8	*85*
23	♗f1	*95*	♗f8	*95*
24	♖d2	*101*	♕b8	*98*
25	♕b1	*104*	♗a8	*100*
26	b4	*109*	♗b7	*103*

27	ab	*115*

The longest wait for a capture in all the games the two K's have played together. Perhaps even a record for world title matches.

27	...		ab	*105*
28	♖ed1	*117*	♕c7	*110*
29	♖c1	*125*		

The grandmasters thought 29 c4 would guarantee White the initiative – it's hard for Black to put together a good counter-plan.

29	...		♗g7	*120*
30	♖cd1	*129*		

30 c4 or 30 de followed by c4 looks more dangerous.

30	...		♖cd8	*124*
31	de	*134*	de	*124*
32	♖xd8	*134*	♖xd8	*126*

| 33 | ♖xd8 | *134* | ♘xd8 | *126* |
| 34 | c4 | *135* | | |

After so much simplification, 34 c4 is less effective.

| 34 | ... | | bc | *129* |
| 35 | ♗xc4 | *135* | ♘e8 | *131* |

Maybe 35 ... ♗c8 and ... ♗e6.

36	♕a2	*140*	♘d6	*131*
37	♗b3	*140*	♘b5	*133*
38	h4	*140*		

Finally opening hostilities on the kingside, but Black's . . .

| 38 | ... | | ♘d4 | *143* |

. . . greatly improved Karpov's position. Of 38 ... ♘d4 Bronstein (Challenger in 1951) said: "In such positions Black dreams of making this move".

| 39 | ♗xd4 | *141* | ed | *143* |
| 40 | h5 | *141* | ♕e7 | *147* |

Now Kasparov played the sharpest possible reply, still in the first session.

| 41 | ♕d2 | *152* | c5 | *148* |
| 42 | ♕c2 | *152* | | |

Karpov now sealed . . .

| 42 | ... | | cb | *152* |

On resumption there followed . . .

| 43 | hg+ | *153* | | |

Much better than 43 ♕c4 gh 44 ♘xd4 h4 45 ♘df5 ♕g5, or 44 ♘xh5 ♗xe4 45 ♘xg7 ♗xf3.

43	...		fg	*153*
44	♕c4	*153*	h5	*153*
45	e5!	*153*		

Absolutely not 45 ♘xd4 ♗xe4 46 ♘xe4 ♕xe4 47 ♕g8+ ♔h6 48 ♕xd8 ♕e1+ 49 ♔h2 ♗e5+!.

45 e5! is the very best and Karpov eventually found the correct reply. If 45 ... h4 then 46 ♘h5! is very good: 46 ... ♗xf3 47 ♕g8+ ♔h6 48 ♘xg7 ♕xg7 49 ♕xd8, or 46 ... gh? 47 ♕g8+ and ♗c2.

45	...		♗xf3	*187*
46	gf	*153*	♗xe5	*187*
47	f4!!	*154*		

Sacrificing a third pawn. If 47 ... ♗g7 then 48 f5 g5 49 ♕g8+ ♔h6 50 f6 ♕xf6 51 ♗c2.

47	...		♗xf4	*197*
48	♕g8+	*155*	♔h6	*197*
49	♗c2	*155*	♕g7!	*199*

If 49 ... ♕f6 then 50 ♘e4. Karpov jettisons a piece to hold the draw.

50	♕xd8	*155*	♗xg3	*199*
51	fg	*155*	♕e5	*199*
52	♕f8+	*156*	♔g5	*199*
53	♔g2	*157*	**Draw Agreed**	

It will be perpetual check.

| Karpov | 0 ½ ½ 1 1 ½ ½ ½ ½ | 5 |
| Kasparov | 1 ½ ½ 0 0 ½ ½ ½ ½ | 4 |

GAME TEN, 28-29 September

The tenth game ended in a draw as Kasparov escaped from a critical situation by means of a stunning series of sacrifices.

The opening was a variation of the Sicilian Defence already used in game 2, but Karpov improved his play from that earlier game. By move 21 the World Champion appeared to be exerting a paralysing grip on the entire Black position. At that point, however, Kasparov struck back with an amazing pawn sacrifice. Kasparov's 25th move – a retreat with his queen – was also particularly fine and extremely difficult to foresee. Karpov surmounted the first wave of Kasparov's counterattack and continued to build up pressure against the Black queenside. Once again, however, Kasparov refused to be driven into passivity and on his 31st move he carried out a second sacrifice, this time of a rook for White's dangerous knight. As a result of this fresh sacrifice he eliminated White's threatening pawns and himself obtained a passed pawn. Nevertheless, the Champion's strong 34th move threatened mate on f7 and Kasparov finally had to seek salvation in an apparently inexplicable sacrifice of his knight. In the final position the pendulum-like series of checks with the black knight ensures a draw by perpetual check.

Karpov-Kasparov
Sicilian Defence

1	e4	0	c5	0
2	♘f3	0	d6	1
3	d4	0	cd	1
4	♘xd4	0	♘f6	1
5	♘c3	0	a6	2
6	♗e2	0	e6	2
7	0-0	0	♗e7	2
8	f4	1	0-0	2
9	♔h1	1	♕c7	3
10	a4	3	♘c6	4
11	♗e3	4	♖e8	4
12	♗g1	8		

Diverging from the 12 ♗f3 of game 2.

12	...		♖b8	18
13	♕d2	18	e5	40
14	♘b3	23	♘a5	45

84

15	♘xa5	45	♕xa5	45
16	♗a7	45	♖a8	45
17	♗e3	45	♕b4	71

17 ... ♕b4 and 18 ... ♗e6 surprised the grandmasters, and when Black's pieces were soon forced back the plan raised criticism from the "GM Council" (a name coined by Taimanov for the press corps of grandmasters). 17 ... ef 18 ♖xf4 ♗e6 is less wild. Holmov proposed 17 ... ♖b8 18 b4!? ♕c7 (18 ... ♕xb4 19 ♖ab1 ♕a5 20 ♗b6 ♘xe4 21 ♘xe4 ♕xd2 22 ♘xd2 ef ±) 19 a5 ♗e6 20 ♗b6 ♕c6; alternatively 19 ♘d5 ♘xd5 20 ed ef 21 ♗xf4 ♗f6 22 ♖a3 b5 23 ab ab 24 ♗e3 ♕e7! with counterplay.

18 ♕d3 55

The analysis team was busy looking at 18 a5, which seems quite good. For example, 18 ... ♘xe4 19 ♘xe4 ♕xe4 20 ♗f3 ♕g6 21 f5 ♕f6 22 ♗d5, or 20 ... ♕f5 21 fe ♕xe5 and now 22 ♗d4 or even 22 ♖ae1.

18	...		♗e6	78
19	f5	59	♗d7	78
20	♖a3	65		

20 a5 allowing 20 ... ♖ec8 21 ♖a3 ♕xb2 22 ♖b3 ♖xc3! 23 ♖xb2 ♖xd3 24 cd ♗c6 is unclear.

20	...		♕a5	84
21	♖b3	65	b5	93

Kasparov's pawn sacrifice seems forced due to the threat of 22 ♗b6, but Kasparov must have seen it way back at move 17, and also at least the idea of ... ♕a8, if not the actual move order. At first, the grandmasters thought White was better and could not understand what Kasparov was up to, but then a group of candidate masters came over and showed the imminent ... ♕a8 idea.

22	ab	66	ab	93
23	♘xb5	68	♗c6	94
24	♗f3	91		

Worth considering is 24 ♘c3 ♖eb8 25 ♖xb8+ ♖xb8 26 ♗c1! ♕a8 27 ♗f3 ♖b4 28 ♖e1 ♖d4 29 ♕e2.

24	...		♖ab8	102
25	c4	97		

If 25 ♘c3 ♖xb3 26 cb ♖b8.

25	...		♕a8!	104

26 ♗g5 *116*

If 26 ♘c7 ♖xb3 27 ♕xb3 ♖b8!.

The last try for an advantage is 26 ♖a3 ♗xe4 27 ♗xe4 ♕xe4 28 ♕xe4 ♘xe4 29 ♖d3. Black should then retreat with 29 ... ♘f6, angling for ... d5 to undermine White's knight on b5.

26 ...		♗xe4	*110*
27	♗xe4 *119*	♘xe4	*110*
28	♗xe7 *124*		

If 28 ♘c7 ♖xb3 29 ♕xb3 ♕a7! with the very tricky threat of ... ♘f2+. Suetin also gives 28 ♘c7 ♘f2+ 29 ♖xf2 ♖xb3 30 ♕xb3 ♕a1+.

28 ...		♖xe7	*111*
29	♖a3 *124*	♕c6	*112*
30	b4 *125*	h5	*120*

Maybe 30 ... h6 is better as then it appears White is fighting for the draw. The text allows a clear draw. Maybe even 30 ... g6 was a possibility for Black.

31 ♘a7 *131*

Best (Taimanov). White now

threatens to consolidate with b5 and ♘c6.

31 ...		♖xa7	*121*
32	♖xa7 *131*	♖xb4	*122*
33	♕f3 *134*	♖xc4	*122*
34	♕xh5 *136*	♘f2+!	*123*
35	♔g1 *136*	♘h3+	*123*

36	♔h1 *136*	♘f2+	*123*
37	♔g1 *136*	**Draw Agreed**	

So Kasparov is back on form and the match is still very much of a fight. Amazingly, Black's impudent knight is immune from capture, viz 35 (or 37) ♖xf2? ♖c1+, or 36 ♕xh3 ♕c5+.

After ten games the score looks like this:

Karpov	0 ½ ½ 1 1 ½ ½ ½ ½ ½	5½
Kasparov	1 ½ ½ 0 0 ½ ½ ½ ½ ½	4½

Recent games have shown Kasparov to be in highly aggressive and sacrificial mood.

GAME ELEVEN, 1 October

A dramatic surprise gives Kasparov his second victory, just when everyone has given up on the position, expecting a short draw.

Karpov continues to arrive late for the games, perhaps to avoid an applause ratings war with his challenger. This time he waited a full three and a half minutes before appearing from backstage. In an obvious display of sportsmanship designed to embarrass the World Champion, Kasparov sat silently, allowing his own clock to run, without making a move.

An event which greatly amused members of the press and perhaps some of the audience occurred when co-Chief Arbiter Vladas Mikenas actually peered behind the curtain after a couple of minutes to look for Karpov. Finally Karpov appeared, they shook hands, Kasparov moved and the demonstrators turned his clock on to three minutes.

The opening, the third Nimzo-Indian of the match, caused some initial excitement in the press room, which today was filled with the largest number of GM observers to date – many, ironically, from the Karpov camp. They included Averbakh and Taimanov (neutrals); Gufeld and Suetin (who writes for *Pravda*); Vaganian, Polugayevsky, Tukmakov, Vasyukov and Georgadze (Karpov camp). Geller from the Karpov camp was also in the press bar with Balashov, who is said here to have broken many of his official links with the World Champion's team. The only visible member of Kasparov's camp was Vladimirov. By move 20 this assembled group of GMs had given up analysing and pronounced the game a draw. Everybody began to relax, waiting for the inevitable, and started analysing earlier variations. The fact that play had entered the fifth hour with only twenty moves made only increased the likelihood of a draw. Presumably Karpov began to relax too, for after Kasparov had set a simple but cunning trap he replied very quickly and fell right into it.

Having played his previous moves in a slow and laboured way, Kasparov tugged at his collar and tie, peered into the audience, and then flashed out his 23 ♛xd7!!. The GM room was stunned and everybody turned to stare at the monitor screen.

Karpov resigned two moves later, after some minutes' thought. There was a huge burst of applause as the crowd stood up, and some even cheered. After a brief handshake Kasparov quickly left the stage, but Karpov remained for about a minute, sorting out his scoresheet, while one segment of the crowd began to chant "Garri, Garri". The noise went on for four minutes. As Frank Guiral of *Prensa Latina* wrote: "They were still applauding as the two players drove away down Gorky Street".

Kasparov-Karpov
Nimzo-Indian Defence

1	d4	3	♘f6	0
2	c4	3	e6	0
3	♘c3	3	♗b4	2
4	♘f3	4	0-0	6
5	♗g5	4	c5	8

Clearly not content with his opening position from game 7.

6	e3	5	cd	10
7	ed	7	h6	13
8	♗h4	8	d5	16
9	♖c1	32	dc	28
10	♗xc4	32	♘c6	29
11	0-0	34	♗e7	29

Curiously the position has transposed into the game Korchnoi-Karpov (9), Merano 1981. We say "curiously" because there is the difference that here White is to move rather than Black! In fact, Karpov has mislaid a tempo, a tempo he used to play ... ♘h5 in that earlier game.

12	♖e1	41	b6	46

13	a3	65

Gufeld gives 13 d5!? ♘xd5 14 ♗xd5 ed 15 ♛xd5 ♗xh4 16 ♛xc6 ♗g4 17 ♘xh4 ♛xh4 18 ♘d5 ±. Better is 15 ... ♛xd5 16 ♘xd5 ♗xh4 17 ♘xh4 ♘d4 =. If 15 ♘d4?! ♗xh4 16 ♘xc6 ♗xf2+! and ... ♛f6+.

13	...	♗b7	50
14	♗g3	65

More accurate is 14 ♗a2, maintaining the pin on Black's king's knight.

14	...		♖c8	68
15	♗a2	67	♗d6	92
16	d5	90		

A more enduring try is 16 ♗h4 (striving to re-establish the pin), e.g. 16 ... ♗e7 17 ♛d3 ♘d5 18 ♘xd5 ♗xh4 19 ♗b1 g6 20 ♘f4 ±, but not 20 ♖xe6 ♘e5!!. Or 16 ♗h4 g5 17 ♗g3 (back again) 17 ... ♗xg3 18 hg g4 19 ♘e5 ♛xd4 20 ♘xf7!? (Taimanov) with complications that should favour White.

16	...		♘xd5	94
17	♘xd5	90	♗xg3	94

| 18 | hg | 93 | ed | 94 |
| 19 | ♗xd5 | 93 | ♕f6 | 104 |

White has more freedom of action, but can he win?

| 20 | ♕a4 | 114 | ♖fd8 | 107 |
| 21 | ♖cd1 | 132 | ♖d7 | 119 |

Not 21 ... ♕xb2 22 ♗xc6 ♖xd1 23 ♗xb7!. But Kasparov personally told us that the best defence is 21 ... ♖c7!.

| 22 | ♕g4 | 139 | ♖cd8? | 119 |

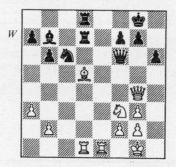

Karpov relaxes, thinking the danger is past, but this permits a deadly combination. After 22 ... ♖dc7 then 23 ♘h4! keeps White

well on top. Black should play 22 ... ♖dd8! but 23 b4 is at least ±. Strangely, Kasparov told us that he had been expecting this "reflex-action" mistake.

23	♕xd7!!	139	♖xd7	119
24	♖e8+	139	♔h7	119
25	♗e4+	139	**Black resigns**	

25 ... g6 26 ♖xd7 ♗a6 27 ♗xc6 ♕xc6 28 ♖xf7 mate.

The combination is highly reminiscent of Alekhine-Colle, Paris 1925:

1 ♕xd7!! ♖xd7 2 ♖e8+ ♔h7 3 ♖cc8 ♖d8 4 ♖exd8 1-0.

| Karpov | 0 | ½ | ½ | 1 | 1 | ½ | ½ | ½ | ½ | ½ | 0 | 5½ |
| Kasparov | 1 | ½ | ½ | 0 | 0 | ½ | ½ | ½ | ½ | ½ | 1 | 5½ |

"While much of modern chess has become dry and technical, Kasparov plays in a way spectators appreciate – he hunts the king with unrestrained ferocity." – Dominic Lawson, *Financial Times*

GAME TWELVE, 3 October

Another impressive game from the Challenger, who produced a stunning theoretical novelty on move 8 of the well-known Taimanov Sicilian to hold the draw easily with the Black pieces. This draw even made the front page of the *Times*.

Karpov did not take a much predicted time-out and was now expected to go in hard with the White pieces to regain some momentum as the match reaches the halfway stage. However, with the use of his innovation Kasparov continues to hold the psychological initiative.

After his loss Karpov broke with his policy of arriving late, entering the stage very shortly after Kasparov. The applause was equally loud for both players, but the Challenger's supporters, cheered by their man's victory, went on longer and broke into rhythmic clapping.

The game also marked the reappearance in the press centre of Josef Dorfman, one of Kasparov's chiefs and his usual representative at the analysis table, who wandered in, tight-lipped but cheerful, shortly after the innovation. He hadn't been seen since the second session of game 9. In fact, only Krogius, Taimanov and Gufeld were there to witness 8 ... d5, but this small group, and especially the eponymous Taimanov, were busily involved in heated analysis of this new move.

After 8 ...d5, Kasparov looked out into the audience with a bored expression on his face and Dorfman commented: "I've been working hard, I'm quite tired". Gufeld then turned to Dorfman and said, "Where have you been?", and added: "I can see it in your eyes, you know everything, it's all home analysis".

While Karpov thought, Kasparov flicked out his moves quickly and spent a long time away from the board walking around backstage. He only really sat and thought properly after Karpov's 15th, choosing a safe reply that led to a draw a few moves later.

Karpov-Kasparov
Sicilian Taimanov

1	e4	0	c5	2
2	♘f3	0	e6	2
3	d4	0	cd	2
4	♘xd4	0	♘c6	3
5	♘b5	2	d6	3
6	c4	3	♘f6	3
7	♘1c3	3	a6	3
8	♘a3	3	d5!?	4

Boldly playing the very move that White's system with 6 c4 is expressly designed to prevent! Their earlier game (and indeed many other Karpov games with White) had continued with the more passive 8 ... ♗e7 9 ♗e2 0-0 10 0-0 b6, setting up a "hedgehog".

9	ed	16	ed	4
10	cd	18	♘b4	5
11	♗c4	28	♗g4	7

If now 12 ♕d4 b5 13 ♗b3 ♗c5! 14 ♕e5+ ♔f8 with excellent coun-

terplay, e.g. 15 0-0 ♘d3 16 ♕g3 ♘xc1 17 ♖axc1 ♗d6 and ... b4. Alternatively, White can sacrifice a piece, but this is very dangerous since Kasparov would obviously have analysed such lines: 12 ♕d4 b5 13 0-0 bc 14 ♗g5 ♘bxd5 15 ♘xd5 ♕xd5 16 ♗xf6 ♕xd4 17 ♗xd4 ♗xa3!. Also, 14 ... ♗e6!? 15 ♗xf6 gf 16 ♕e4 ♘xd5 17 ♖ad1 f5 18 ♕e5 ♕f6 19 ♖xd5 ♕xe5 20 ♖xe5 and now either ... ♗xa3 or ... ♗g7. Inadequate, however is 12 ♕d4 ♗d6? 13 0-0 ♘c6 14 ♕e3+ (14 dc? ♗xh2+) 14 ... ♘e5 15 f4 ♕e7! 16 fe ♗c5 17 ef!! ♗xe3+ 18 ♔h1 and White wins.

12	♗e2	36		

Or 12 f3 ♗f5 13 0-0 ♗c5+ 14 ♔h1 0-0 15 ♗g5 b5 16 ♗e2 ♘bxd5 17 ♘xd5 ♕xd5 18 ♗xf6 ♕xd1 19 ♖axd1 gf 20 ♖d5 ♗xa3! =.

12	...		♗xe2	7
13	♕xe2+	40	♕e7	7
14	♗e3	58	♘bxd5	8
15	♘c2	63	♘xe3	17

Even stronger is 15 ... ♘xc3 16 bc g6 followed by ... ♗g7.

16	♘xe3	63	♕e6	17
17	0-0	70	♗c5	18
18	♖fe1	74	0-0	21

Draw Agreed

Kasparov told us that "his gambit" is sound and he would play it again.

Karpov	0 ½ ½ 1 1 ½ ½ ½ ½ ½ ½ 0 ½	6
Kasparov	1 ½ ½ 0 0 ½ ½ ½ ½ ½ ½ 1 ½	6

Game THIRTEEN, 8 October

Just before this game an article appeared in *Der Spiegel*, which was speedily picked up by other organs of the press, alleging that Karpov had earned 446,000 US dollars for endorsing Hong Kong chess computers. However, *Spiegel* went on to claim that Helmut Jungwirth, Karpov's European "agent", had failed to deliver the funds to him. Jungwirth, a chess and TV journalist of Hanover Broadcasting, is alleged to be under suspicion of diverting the money which should have been paid to Karpov. *Spiegel* also implicated Kinzel, the Jury Chairman, and Campomanes as acting on Karpov's behalf to retrieve what was owed. *Spiegel* further stated that a warrant had been issued in West Germany for Jungwirth's arrest. Under Soviet law, Karpov would have been bound to transfer this money and receive certificates for a portion of it.

"Soviet grandmasters were describing the affair as a 'scandal', and one raised the question of whether Karpov might suffer a heavy tax liability in the West." – *Financial Times*.

One can only speculate on the effect of these allegations (whether founded or not) on Karpov's morale at this stage of the match, as the news became common currency in Moscow chess circles.

In the game Karpov survived initial difficulties. Kasparov obtained good compensation for a pawn sacrificed on move 10 but missed his way eight moves later, allowing a neat simplifying manoeuvre (19 ... ♕h6!). The audience was very noisy today and in unprecedented fashion certain sections broke into premature applause after Kasparov's 13th move.

Kasparov-Karpov				2	c4	*1*	e6	*0*
Nimzo-Indian Defence				3	♘c3	*1*	♗b4	*0*
				4	♘f3	*1*	c5	*1*
1	d4	*1*	♘f6	*0*	5	g3	*1*	♘c6	*1*

92

6	♗g2	*1*	♘e4	*3*
7	♗d2	*2*	♗xc3	*10*
8	bc	*3*	0-0	*12*
9	0-0	*3*	f5!?	*18*

May be a new move. Taimanov's new book on the Nimzo-Indian, just out in Moscow, gives 9 ... d6!.

10 ♗e3! *37*

An excellent move, found after long thought. White must gambit the pawn to stay active. If now 10 ... d6 11 ♕d3 followed by ♘d2 and e4 is possible. Alternatively, 10 ... b6 11 ♕d3 ♗a6 12 dc ♘xc5 13 ♗xc5 bc 14 ♖fd1 ♖f7 15 ♘d2 ♖c8 16 f4 ♘a5 17 e4! with initiative.

10	...		♘xc3	*65*
11	♕d3	*55*	cd	*68*
12	♘xd4	*57*	♘e4	*69*
13	c5!?	*70*		

This brought clapping from the over-enthusiastic audience, but perhaps 13 ♖fd1 is stronger, accumulating d-file energy.

13	...		♘xd4	*98*

13 ... ♘xc5?? 14 ♘xc6 wins.

14	♗xd4	*74*	b6!	*106*

The best way to relieve his cramp.

15	♗xe4	*80*	fe	*106*
16	♕xe4	*80*	♗a6	*106*
17	cb	*82*		

Bronstein told us: "A Bronstein would never play this move, releasing Black's queen's rook. Correct is 17 ♖ac1!".

17	...		ab	*106*

Kasparov now has an edge, which he should, at least, have been able to maintain till adjournment. 18 ♕e5? is wrong. Maybe 18 ♖ab1, 18 ♕g4 or, as generally pushed in the press room, 18 a4! to fix b6 as a weakness.

18 ♕e5? *100*

Now the game peters out, and 19 ... ♕h6! is an outstanding defence.

18	...		♕f6	*114*
19	♕e3	*102*	♕h6!	*118*
20	♕xh6	*102*	gh	*118*
21	♖fe1	*103*	♗c4	*120*
22	a3	*104*	b5	*121*
23	♖ad1	*106*	♖f5	*124*
24	♗b2	*112*	♖d5	*125*

Draw Agreed

Karpov	0	½	½	1	1	½	½	½	½	½	½	0	½	½	**6½**
Kasparov	1	½	½	0	0	½	½	½	½	½	½	1	½	½	**6½**

GAME FOURTEEN, 10 October

The 14th game was drawn after a keenly contested and innovative game. Both sides played the opening moves cautiously and slowly, and after twelve moves Karpov appeared to have a dominating knight in the centre of the board. Kasparov forced the exchange of this knight by subtle play and then proceeded to launch a violent counterattack with queen and knight against Karpov's exposed kingside. This obliged the Champion to exchange queens and accept the disadvantage of doubled pawns. Again Kasparov sought to seize the initiative by marching forward with his d-pawn, but by means of further simplification the Champion avoided all difficulties. The exchange of rooks neutralised Black's passed pawn and in the final position the inevitable exchange of White's bishop for Black's knight would leave a clearly drawn ending of opposite bishops.

Karpov-Kasparov
Sicilian Taimanov

1	e4	*1*	c5	*1*
2	♘f3	*1*	e6	*2*
3	d4	*1*	cd	*2*
4	♘xd4	*1*	♘c6	*2*
5	♘c3	*3*		

For this game Karpov avoids the game 12 continuation.

5	...		d6	*3*
6	g4!?	*4*		

In this position a new move. The normal Keres Attack variation is with g4 against ... ♘f6. The text looks aggressive, but evidently loosens White's kingside. There is a conceptual precedent for it in a game by one of Karpov's seconds, Zaitsev-Vogt, USSR 1980: 1 e4 c5 2 ♘f3 e6 3 d4 cd 4 ♘xd4 d6 5 ♘c3 ♗e7 6 g4!? a6 7 ♗e3 b5 8 ♗g2 ♗b7 9 0-0 h5!. We found this in Kasparov's Batsford book on the Scheveningen! Naturally, his team would also subject the games of the Champion's aids to close scrutiny.

94

6	...		h6	24
7	h4	8	a6	38

Kasparov had been moving slowly until now, but after this Karpov stopped for a lengthy period of cogitation.

8	♗g2	37	♗e7	60
9	♗e3	46		

If now 9 ... ♗xh4? 10 ♘xc6 bc 11 e5 d5 12 ♕d2 and Black cannot complete his development.

9	...		♘xd4	62
10	♕xd4	48	e5	62
11	♕d1	57	♗e6	68
12	♘d5	61	♖c8	68
13	c3	70	♘f6	77
14	♘xe7	78	♕xe7	87

14 ... ♔xe7 is very interesting, e.g. 15 g5 ♘g4 16 ♗d2 hg 17 hg ♖xh1+ 18 ♗xh1 ♕b6 19 ♕e2 ♖h8 20 ♗f3 ♖h2! attacking f2. Stronger is 15 ♗f3!.

15	g5	85	hg	90
16	hg	85		

If 16 ♗xg5 ♕c7! 17 ♗xf6 gf followed by ... ♔e7 and ... ♖cg8 with counterplay.

16	...		♖xh1+	90
17	♗xh1	85	♘g4	93

Risky; safer is 17 ... ♘d7 18 ♕h5 ♘f8.

18	♗d2	85	♕f8!	93

Introducing a highly original counterattack manoeuvre.

19	♕f3	98	♕h8	96

20	♗g2	102	♕h4	100
21	b3	105		

To stop ... ♗c4.

21	...		d5!	112

If now 22 ed ♗xd5 23 ♕xd5 ♕xf2+ 24 ♔d1 ♖d8 wins. Karpov now wriggles out of Black's initiative by deft simplification.

22	♕g3!	105	♕xg3	112
23	fg	105	♖d8	112
24	♔e2	107	♔e7	114
25	♗c1!	113		

Looks odd, but Kasparov told us it was the best. He also pointed out the neat variation 25 ♖h1? de 26 ♗xe4 ♘f2!! winning.

25	...		d4	124
26	♗a3+	120	♔e8	128
27	cd	123	ed	128
28	♖h1	123	♘e5	130
29	♖h8+	125	♔d7	131
30	♖xd8+	125	♔xd8	131
31	♗b2	127	♗g4+	131
32	♔d2	127	♘f3+	133

Draw Agreed

Karpov	0 ½ ½ 1 1 ½ ½ ½ ½ ½ ½ 0 ½ ½ ½	7
Kasparov	1 ½ ½ 0 0 ½ ½ ½ ½ ½ ½ 1 ½ ½ ½	7

GAME FIFTEEN, 12 October

A minor triumph for Karpov who had apparently out-analysed Kasparov's team in the opening. Karpov improved on game 48 from last time and after Black's 8th move Kasparov sat for 46 minutes, at times hunched over the board folding and unfolding his arms, at others rocking back and forth nervously in his chair.

After his 16th move, regaining the pawn, Kasparov visibly relaxed, while it was now the Champion's turn to sit glued to the board, seeking the perfect route to equality. Having made his 18th Kasparov tried to leave the stage but could not find the gap in the curtains to the rest area. He fumbled with the drapes for a while, to the audience's amusement. On his return a draw was soon agreed.

Kasparov-Karpov
Petroff Defence

1	e4	1	e5	1
2	♘f3	1	♘f6	1
3	♘xe5	1	d6	1
4	♘f3	1	♘xe4	1
5	d4	1	d5	3
6	♗d3	1	♘c6	5
7	0-0	1	♗g4	9
8	c4	1	♘f6	10
9	♘c3	47	♗xf3	12
10	♕xf3	47	♘xd4	12
11	♖e1+	62	♗e7	12
12	♕d1	62		

A theoretical novelty over Lobron-Karpov, Hanover 1983, where 12 ♕g3 was tried without success. We had the impression that Kasparov had analysed this position some time ago but could not perfectly recall his analysis.

12	...		♘e6	16
13	cd	65	♘xd5	16
14	♗b5+	65	c6	16
15	♘xd5	65	cb	16

96

16 ♕b3?! *80*

This merely regains the pawn and leads to a sterile wasteland. Not **16 ♗f4?** ♘xf4! 17 ♖xe7+ ♔f8 18 ♖e5 ♕d6 19 ♕d4 f6 and White is in deep trouble. But **16 ♕h5!** is worth examination, e.g. 16 ... 0-0 17 ♗e3 ♗g5 18 ♖ad1 ♗xe3 19 ♖xe3 ♕g5 20 ♕xg5 ♘xg5 21 f4 ♘e6 22 f5 ♘c5 23 b4!. For a pawn Black's knight is driven offside and White's rooks can invade the seventh rank.

16 ...   0-0 *27*

Of course, not 16 ... a6 17 ♗e3 0-0 18 ♖ad1 and Black's men are slaughtered in their beds.

17 ♘xe7+	*83*	**♕xe7**	*27*
18 ♕xb5	*83*	**a6**	*34*
19 ♕b3	*86*	**♖fd8**	*40*
20 ♗e3	*87*	**♖ac8**	*47*
21 ♖ac1	*87*	**h6**	*61*
22 h3	*105*	**♘d4!**	*77*

Draw Agreed

23 ♗xd4 ♖xc1 24 ♖xc1 ♖xd4 is dead level.

Karpov	0 ½ ½ 1 1 ½ ½ ½ ½ ½ 0 ½ ½ ½ ½	7½
Kasparov	1 ½ ½ 0 0 ½ ½ ½ ½ ½ 1 ½ ½ ½ ½	7½

On 14 October co-author Ray Keene participated as part of the panel in a public seminar, at Moscow University on Lenin Hills, devoted to whether chess is a sport, art or science. First came a film based around the original Karpov-Kasparov match. Jon Tisdall appeared on screen asserting somewhat tentatively, "It's a sport", and then co-author David Goodman opining, "It's a game *and* a sport". The whole film was in colour, with a lively, racy tone – shots of smiling children in the park playing chess, *babushkas* (Russian grandmothers) heatedly analysing the latest nuances of opening theory . . . that is, until the part which covered the match termination. Then came a switch to funereal black and white stills, with mugshots of Karpov, Kasparov, Campomanes – all looking very grim indeed. The word *nichya* ('draw') seemed to flash onto the screen, then out like a sombre leitmotif. At the subsequent question-and-answer session Keene was posed questions about Nunn, Short, Fischer and even Korchnoi. A prominent member of the audience was Florencio Campomanes Jr, the FIDE President's son, who is studying philology at Moscow University. The evening concluded with a display of prestidigitation by Arutyan Akopian, an Armenian magician and close friend and supporter of the late World Champion, Tigran Petrosian. In full view of the audience surrounding him on three sides, and directly in front of various FIDE officials, Akopian succeeded in shredding a newspaper and reassembling it again, in a split second – not the first time an accomplished trickster has pulled the wool over FIDE's eyes.

GAME SIXTEEN, 15 October

An amazing display from Kasparov, who completely paralysed the World Champion to win this important game. As he had indicated to us a few days before, Kasparov believes his Sicilian Gambit to be sound, and he demonstrated his faith by using it again to secure a crushing victory.

Karpov glanced casually and confidently into the audience after his fifth and eighth moves, but Kasparov was noticeably unruffled and flicked out 8 ... d5 after less than thirty seconds' thought. The crowd waited expectantly for White's improvement over game 12, but instead it was Kasparov who produced the real surprise. The Challenger rested backstage while Karpov thought for six minutes over his 12th move and sixteen over his 13th. Downstairs in the press bar members of the Karpov camp sat in a semi-circle around the TV monitors. It was more than clear, from the looks on their faces, that Karpov had been completely out-prepared.

Meanwhile, four flights higher in the grandmaster room, Dorfman kept his hands firmly on the table, refusing to take part in the feverish analysis of the position. Instead he wandered over to the authors and said: "I feel there will be a result today. White cannot draw after 13 ♗f3".

Kasparov's moves 16 to 19 convinced experts that Black stood better, and Karpov's team began to slowly drift upstairs. Two analysis groups quickly formed. One contained Dorfman, Sveshnikov and Polugayevsky, the other Taimanov, Vasyukov and Chiburdanidze. Asked his opinion of the position after the brilliant 23 ... ♘d7!, Sveshnikov, a member of Karpov's analysis team, muttered "Scandal".

The tension was overwhelming in the Hall with both players retiring backstage after nearly every move. Karpov became more and more restricted, and as he tried to break out, Dorfman, sitting on the side of the White pieces, kept winning the position for Kasparov in analysis with Polugayevsky. The tactics were massively in Black's favour and as we entered the last hour the GM room began to swarm with people. Karpov's time was ticking away – fifteen minutes for eleven moves, five for eight, and finally he was only left with two minutes.

The crowded GM room turned to face the TV monitor while others rushed onto the balcony to watch the stage. Dorfman, who sensed very well what was coming, was so nervous as he viewed the stage that he was unable to calculate the winning variation, and kept cursing, "Yes, that wins . . . no, it doesn't work . . . ". Suddenly it was all over and the entire Hall rose to their feet applauding, with some cheering loudly. There was the usual perfunctory handshake and Kasparov immediately left the stage, shortly followed by Karpov. It had been no mean achievement for Jon Tisdall of Reuters, who had predicted a Black victory 40 minutes before the game began. As for the chess, game 16 was widely hailed as the best the two have played so far.

Karpov-Kasparov
Sicilian Taimanov

1	e4	1	c5	0
2	♘f3	1	e6	1
3	d4	1	cd	1
4	♘xd4	1	♘c6	1
5	♘b5	2	d6	1
6	c4	2	♘f6	1
7	♘1c3	3	a6	1
8	♘a3	3	d5	2

A roar went up in the GM room as the Kasparov Gambit was repeated. It was followed by a crash that sounded very much like a fist hitting a table, and then some shouting. It seems a number of experts were sure that the move from game 12 was merely a bluff and would not be repeated. But now Kasparov's unhesitating eagerness to go into the variation again was surely more than just bravado.

9	cd	4

A little joke from Karpov, who reverses the order of captures on d5.

9	...		ed	2
10	ed	4	♘b4	3
11	♗e2	4		

Karpov's new move, wheeled out quickly after a week and a half of preparation, but after Kasparov replied . . .

11	...		♗c5	3

. . . Karpov looked puzzled and sank into deep thought. What Karpov's camp had evidently looked at were positions resulting from 11 ... ♘bxd5 12 ♘xd5 ♘xd5 13 0-0 and ♗f3, where White could claim a small advantage. They had probably dismissed other alternatives as unlikely.

12	0-0	10	0-0	4
13	♗f3	26		

A very natural move. 13 &g5 ♘bxd5 14 ♘xd5 ♛xd5 15 &xf6 ♛xd1 16 ♖fxd1 gf is level. So Karpov tries to cling to his extra pawn, but in the process underestimates the significance of the d3 square.

| 13 | ... | | &f5 | 5 |
| 14 | &g5 | 28 | ♖e8 | 21 |

Moscow grandmasters were raving about 14 ... &d3 15 ♖e1 ♘g4 16 &xd8 ♘xf2 17 &e7 ♘xd1+ but 17 ♛d2! refutes.

| 15 | ♛d2 | 38 | b5 | 32 |
| 16 | ♖ad1 | 52 | ♘d3 | 37 |

This piece starts out as a knight but shortly transforms into a monstrous centralised octopus, tentacles grasping out in all directions, hovering over the key squares in White's position.

| 17 | ♘ab1 | 60 | | |

Trying to regroup in the centre. In reply to 17 ♘c2 Suetin suggests 17 ... ♘xb2 18 ♘e3 &xe3 19 fe ♘xd1 20 &xd1 ♛d7.

| 17 | ... | | h6 | 41 |
| 18 | &h4 | 66 | b4 | 45 |

Simultaneously imprisoning the knight on b1 while forcing the other to the side of the board well away from the action. Of course, if 19 ♘e2 then ... g5-g4 will win a piece.

19	♘a4	77	&d6	50
20	&g3	84	♖c8	76
21	b3	89	g5!!	90

Coupled with move 23 this plan deserves a double exclamation mark. Kasparov's fearless advance sent a buzz through the audience, and some spectators left the Hall to analyse the position.

| 22 | &xd6 | 106 | ♛xd6 | 91 |
| 23 | g3 | 106 | | |

If 23 &e2 then 23 ... ♘f4 followed by ... ♖c2.

| 23 | ... | | ♘d7! | 102 |

The most difficult move of the game. Black frees the f6 square for his queen and shows White that if one knight on d3 is somehow removed it can always be replaced by the other.

| 24 | &g2 | 110 | ♛f6 | 107 |

With ♘b2 cut out White is fast running out of moves. It's remarkable how two knights and two rooks are kept out of play by only one knight on d3 and one pawn on b4.

25	a3	114	a5	108
26	ab	114	ab	108
27	♛a2	115		

White is almost in zugzwang. It is incredible that Kasparov has done this to the World Champion on a nearly full board.

27 ...   **♗g6**   *112*

At first GMs were looking at 27 ... ♘f4 but Suetin, writing in *Pravda*, gives 28 gf ♖c2 29 ♘b2 ♖xb2 30 fg hg and now 31 ♕a4.

28 d6   *127*   **g4**   *123*
29 ♕d2   *135*   **♔g7**   *126*
30 f3   *138*

Karpov decides to break out of the straitjacket. If he had chosen to sit it out, Black would most probably have increased the pressure with ideas like ... h5-h4 and ... ♖h8.

30 ...   **♕xd6**   *127*
31 fg   *140*

Or 31 ♘b2 ♕d4+ 32 ♔h1 ♕xb2 33 ♕xb2 ♘xb2 34 ♖xd7 ♗d3 35 ♖g1 ♖c2 36 fg ♖ee2 37 ♖e4 ♗b5 38 ♖d6 (to stop ... ♗c6) 38 ... ♘d3 39 h3 ♘e1 and wins.

31 ...   **♕d4+**   *129*

32 ♔h1   *140*   **♘f6**   *134*

Bringing the second knight in for the kill as Karpov's time-trouble worsened.

33 ♖f4   *146*   **♘e4**   *137*
34 ♕xd3   *148*

If 34 ♕a2 then 34 ... ♘df2+.

34 ...   **♘f2+**   *137*
35 ♖xf2   *149*

Or 35 ♔g1 ♘h3+ 36 ♔h1 ♕xd3 37 ♖xd3 ♖e1+ winning everything.

35 ...   **♗xd3**   *137*
36 ♖fd2   *149*   **♕e3**   *139*
37 ♖xd3   *149*   **♖c1**   *140*
38 ♘b2   *149*

If 38 ♖xe3 ♖xd1+ and ... ♖xe3.

38 ...   **♕f2**   *140*
39 ♘d2   *149*

White's knights fall over each other scurrying back to the centre. Fastest now is 39 ... ♖e2.

39 ...   **♖xd1+**   *140*
40 ♘xd1   *149*   **♖e1+**   *140*
Karpov resigned. It's mate after 41 ♘f1 ♖xf1+ 42 ♗xf1 ♕xf1.

Karpov	0	½	½	1	1	½	½	½	½	½	0	½	½	½	½	0	7½
Kasparov	1	½	½	0	0	½	½	½	½	½	1	½	½	½	½	1	8½

GAME SEVENTEEN, 17 October

Karpov came out fighting after his loss and held the draw easily with Black in a mysterious game that left grandmasters unable to predict many of the moves. Although Karpov must really be feeling the pressure, it was Kasparov who seemed nervous today, now that he was in the lead. He certainly gave some of his supporters heartaches by creating the normally very weak tripled pawns on the c-file, combined with spending 80 minutes over moves ten and eleven. However, after Karpov refused to take the sacrificed pawn and made space on the queenside to develop his pieces, predictions were for an early draw.

After the game Karpov appeared to try and engage the Challenger in conversation, but Kasparov replied briefly – no more than a few words – and quickly left the stage.

FIDE President Campomanes was in attendance after arriving back in Moscow today from opening the Candidates' tournament in Montpellier.

Kasparov-Karpov
Nimzo-Indian Defence

1	d4	2	♘f6	0
2	c4	2	e6	0
3	♘c3	2	♗b4	1
4	♘f3	2	c5	6
5	g3	2	♘c6	6
6	♗g2	2	♘e4	6
7	♗d2	2	♗xc3	13
8	bc	2	0-0	14
9	0-0	2	♘a5!	20

Karpov's new try. After 10 ♗f4

d5! 11 cd ed (11 ... ♘xc3 12 ♕d2 ♘xd5 13 dc ±) 12 dc ♗e6 Black is OK. Kasparov seemed utterly perplexed by this really quite natural knight sortie, and went into a trance over his next two moves.

10 dc 45 ♕c7 26

Tripled pawns on the c-file have been rare in world title matches since the Botvinnik-Smyslov clashes of the mid 1950s. Karpov looks set now for a smooth exploitation of

102

♘b5!. Also dangerous is 14 ... ♕xc5 15 ♘b3 ♕b5 16 ♕c7 d5 17 e4!. Karpov sensibly steers for consolidation and exchanges.

15	♘b3	90	♖b8	48
16	♕d4	97	b6	50
17	f4	98	♘f7	51
18	♖fd1	100	♖d8	54
19	c4	105	♗b7	64
20	♗xb7	106	♖xb7	68
21	cb	106	♖xb6	74
22	c5	108	♖c6	78
23	♖ac1	112	d5	92

White's weaknesses, but Kasparov's spoiling tactics never allow him to settle down.

11 ♘d4   82

Ingenious but unsound is 11 ♗f4? ♕xc5 12 ♘g5 ♘xg5 13 ♗d6 ♕f5! and White will not have enough.

Now the position burns out. Gufeld was all for the cavalier 23 ... e5, but surely 24 ♕c4 ♔f8 25 e3 is at least ±.

11	...		♘xd2	28
12	♕xd2	82	♘xc4	28
13	♕g5	82	f6	39
14	♕f4	86	♘e5	43

If 14 ... e5? 15 ♗d5+ ♔h8 16·

24	cd	114	♖xd6	93
25	♕e3	115	♖xd1+	100
26	♖xd1	116	g6	101
27	♖c1	119	♖xc1+	112
28	♕xc1	121	♕b6+	114
29	♕c5	122	**Draw Agreed**

Karpov	0	½	½	1	1	½	½	½	½	½	0	½	½	½	½	0	½		**8**
Kasparov	1	½	½	0	0	½	½	½	½	½	1	½	½	½	½	1	½		**9**

Reuters reported: "Sources close to the Champion acknowledged that recent events had weighed on Karpov's mind and the Moscow crowd's support for the young pretender had unnerved him. Karpov's appearance has changed since the first game. He has lost the weight he gained in the six-month interval and again has a frail look, while Kasparov gives the impression of a strong and confident opponent."

Meanwhile, Colonel Viktor Davidovich Baturinsky, the Champion's head of delegation both in this match and in the struggles with Korchnoi, told us that Karpov's tribulations, starting with game 32 in the previous match with Kasparov, "had taken five years off his life".

GAME EIGHTEEN, 22 October

Campomanes was very much in evidence today as, accompanied by his son, the FIDE Vice-President Rafael Tudela and a man from the Philippine embassy he went on a grand tour of the press bar, press room and GM analysis room.

Observers were surprised by the premature draw and some criticised Karpov for not fighting harder with the White pieces, but analysis showed that Kasparov might even stand slightly better after ... ♘d4 and ... ♔h8. It was noticeable that Kasparov spent a great deal of time on accepting Karpov's offer, but with time pressure approaching a draw seemed a fair result.

Karpov-Kasparov					12	♗f3	8	♖b8	4
Sicilian Najdorf/Scheveningen					13	♕d2	12	♗d7	9
					14	♘b3	19		
1	e4	0	c5	1	14 ♕f2 was played in game 2.				
2	♘f3	0	d6	1	14	...		b6	29
3	d4	0	cd	1	15	♗f2	20	♗c8	39
4	♘xd4	0	♘f6	2	16	♗g3	41	♘d7	50
5	♘c3	0	a6	2	17	♖ae1	87	♗b7	72
6	♗e2	0	e6	2	18	e5	90	♖bd8	76
7	0-0	0	♗e7	2	19	♕f2	98	♖f8	77
8	f4	4	0-0	2	20	♗e4	105	de	91
9	♔h1	5	♕c7	2	21	fe	105	♘c5	92
10	a4	5	♘c6	2	22	♘xc5	110	bc	98
11	♗e3	5	♖e8	2	23	♗f4	113	**Draw Agreed**	

Karpov	0	½	½	1	1	½	½	½	½	½	0	½	½	½	½	0	½	½	8½
Kasparov	1	½	½	0	0	½	½	½	½	½	1	½	½	½	½	1	½	½	9½

GAME NINETEEN, 24 October

Kasparov goes two ahead following unprecedented scenes in Moscow's Tchaikovsky Hall, where in a totally won position he reveals his sealed move by actually playing it on the board – to the accompaniment of wild applause from the audience. This is almost certainly the first time an open sealed move has been made in a world title contest, and it is indeed very rare in grandmaster play.

With both players running short of time, Kasparov opens lines against the black king. The balcony is overrun by a semi-circle of GMs, match staff and correspondents, hanging over the edge to watch the action. Karpov makes it to the time control, but it seems clear that Kasparov's 41st move will force immediate resignation. Dorfman turns to co-author David Goodman and says in an excited and hushed tone: " ♖b1 – it's over".

Co-Chief Arbiter Mikenas steps in front of the stage and calls for silence by waving his arms in the air, but he's impotent in the face of the effervescent partisan spectators. Suddenly a man in the audience begins to shout. Such is the tension and confusion in the Hall that accounts vary as to the exact words and translation. Some hear: "Don't give up, Anatoly Yevgenyevich", while others report, "Why play? Resign, Anatoly Yevgenyevich". Then Kasparov thinks for a few more moments, lifts his hand and plays what ought to be the sealed move on the board. There are a couple of seconds' mystery, but the move is recognised in the gallery and the demonstrators move their metal rods up to the giant demonstration boards. As they pick up the queen there is another burst of applause from the crowd and Kasparov strides off the stage quickly and confidently.

That evening, on the nightly chess programme, Alexei Suetin, perhaps unconsciously, does not use the usual title "World Champion" before describing Karpov's moves, but speaks of Black and White instead.

As Kasparov built up a strong position from the opening, Božidar Kažić, a Yugoslav member of FIDE's Executive Council, mentioned that a certain Dr Vladimir Zukhar of Baguio fame was sitting in the audience with his son, in the sixth row. This was a particular surprise, but how could Kažić be sure he was there? "Well, I'm going to meet him in a few minutes", he replied. Kažić returned and reported that Zukhar had also been present for game 7. Zukhar told Kažić he was not working for either camp and was now working away from chess. "Of course you're not working for anyone," Kažić retorted, "Nobody won game 7." Of course, Kasparov's victory had absolutely nothing to do with Zukhar.

Kasparov's supporters seemed worried during the middlegame that their man had lost the thread of the position, but after Kasparov recaptured on e4 Dorfman announced quietly: "I think it's still winning". Two moves later, with eight still to play, Mikenas moved to the board to scrutinise the clocks.

Kasparov's decision to seal openly was described by some present as "a punch in the face because Karpov had failed to resign an utterly hopeless position". Others claimed it was uncouth to seal openly even in a crushing position. Karpov, in fact, resigned by telephone to Mikenas the next morning.

Kasparov-Karpov
Nimzo-Indian Defence

1	d4	1	♘f6 0
2	c4	1	e6 0
3	♘c3	1	♗b4 2
4	♘f3	1	♘e4 5

On the stage the tension was evident. After Karpov played 4 ... ♘e4 he got up and walked around confidently with his hands folded to his chest. The idea appears to be to take Kasparov out of his deep opening preparation and force him to play at the board. Alekhine-A.Olivera, Montevideo

1939, went 4 ... ♗xc3+ 5 bc d6 6 g3 0-0 7 ♗g2 ♘c6 8 0-0 ♕e7 9 ♗a3 e5 10 c5 d5 11 ♘xe5 ♘xe5 12 de ♕xe5 13 c4 ♖d8 14 cd ♘xd5 15 e4 ♕c3 16 ed ♕xa3 17 ♕c2 ♗g4 18 ♖ab1 ♖ab8 19 ♖fe1 ♗h5 20 ♖e3 ♕a5 21 f4 ♖e8 22 ♖xb7 ± and Alekhine soon won. The opening of this game was published in Taimanov's new book on the Nimzo. Had Karpov or Kasparov seen it? The double advance of White's c-pawn is revealing.

| 5 | ♕c2 | 6 | f5 | 5 |
| 6 | g3 | 17 | | |

6 g4!? c5 7 gf ♗xc3+ 8 bc ef 9

♘d2 d5 10 cd ♘xd2 11 ♕xd2 ♕xd5 12 ♖g1 was Borisenko-Evdokimov, correspondence 1962.

6	...	♘c6	16

6 ... b6 7 ♗g2 ♗b7 8 ♘d2 ♗xc3 9 bc ♘d6 10 ♗xb7 ♘xb7 11 e4 0-0 12 0-0 ± Balogh-Keres, correspondence 1937.

7	♗g2	27	0-0	34
8	0-0	32	♗xc3	34
9	bc	32	♘a5	34
10	c5	44	d6	55

10 ... b6 was analysed by GMs in the press centre: 11 ♘d2 (11 c4 ♗b7 or ♗a6) 11 ... ♘xd2 12 ♗xd2 ♗b7 13 c4 ♗xg2 14 ♔xg2 ♘c6 15 d5 ♘e7.

11	c4!	66		

Combined with 12 ♗d2 this is a magnificent conception. If 11 ... dc 12 dc ♘xc5 13 ♗a3 with tremendous compensation.

11	...	b6	68
12	♗d2	85	♘xd2	85
13	♘xd2	87	d5	85

Grandmasters were looking at 13 ... ♖b8 14 c6 ♕e7 15 d5 but we were sure Karpov wouldn't go

into it. Taimanov gives 13 ... d5 as dubious but 13 ... ♗b7 allowing a later c6 looks worse.

14	cd	93	ed	85
15	e3	98		

White has a large positional advantage. Black's bishop is bad, his dark squares are weak and White can play on the queenside. It's hard for Black to organise counterplay.

15	...	♗e6	90

If 15 ... ♗a6 16 ♖fc1 ♘c4 17 ♗f1. If 15 ... b5 16 ♕c3! ♘c4 17 a4.

16	♕c3	101		

Taimanov was confidently predicting that White would shortly stand much better.

16	...	♖f7	97
17	♖fc1	103		

Kasparov walked backwards and forwards on the stage, also looking confident.

17	...	♖b8	102
18	♖ab1	106	♖e7	109
19	a4	110	♗f7	110
20	♗f1	115	h6	115
21	♗d3	119	♕d7	119

The GMs had separated into two groups. Taimanov, Dorfman and Tukmakov formed one, Vasyukov and Polugayevsky the other. Sveshnikov, one of Karpov's closest aides, sat analysing on his own.

22 ♕c2 *125*

Dorfman started to get nervous and said he felt Kasparov was drifting without a plan from moves 22 to 28. At the time he preferred procedures for White based on f4 and ♘f3-e5. Why not, for example, 22 ♘f3? After 22 ... ♘c4 23 ♗xc4 dc 24 ♘e5 Black may have to play 24 ... ♖xe5, which looks desperate.

22 ...   ♗e6 *119*
23 ♗b5 *127* **♕d8** *121*
24 ♖d1 *129* **g5** *127*

Voluntarily undermining his own position in the hope of a wild counterattack.

25 ♘f3 *133* **♖g7** *127*

If 25 ... ♘c4 26 ♗xc4 dc 27 d5!.

26 ♘e5 *134* **f4** *129*
27 ♗f1 *137* **♕f6** *130*
28 ♗g2 *137* **♖d8** *135*
29 e4 *139*

The decisive breakthrough.

29 ...   de *136*
30 ♗xe4 *139* **♖e7** *136*
31 ♕c3 *141* **♗d5** *144*
32 ♖e1 *143* **♔g7** *144*
33 ♘g4 *144* **♕f7** *145*

34 ♗xd5 *145* **♖xd5** *146*
35 ♖xe7 *146* **♕xe7** *146*
36 ♖e1 *147* **♕d8** *148*
37 ♘e5 *148*

White has systematically swapped off all of Black's active pieces. Just compare the position of the respective knights now.

37 ...   ♕f6 *149*

He had to play 37 ... fg.

38 cb *148* **♕xb6** *149*
39 gf *149* **♖xd4?** *149*

A terrible blunder in appalling time trouble, but if 39 ... gf 40 ♔h1 followed by ♖g1+. Alternatively, 39 ... c6 40 fg ♕xd4 41 gh+ wins.

40 ♘f3 *149* **♘b3** *149*
41 ♖b1 *150* **♕f6** *150*
42 ♕xc7+ *152*

The open sealed move. **Karpov resigned**, without resuming, by telephone to the Chief Arbiter of the day, Mikenas. White has a choice of taking Black's rook or knight or trying for a mating attack.

Karpov	0	½	½	1	1	½	½	½	½	½	0	½	½	½	½	0	½	½	0	8½
Kasparov	1	½	½	0	0	½	½	½	½	½	1	½	½	½	½	1	½	½	1	10½

GAME TWENTY, 26-27 October

With a real sense of theatre, in a quiet and uninteresting position, Kasparov ignites the Tchaikovsky Hall by playing an open sealed move for the second game in a row. After defending against Karpov's microscopic but enduring advantage for 25 moves he reaches a position which all GMs describe as "surely drawn". Karpov leaves the stage as Kasparov is sealing. Suddenly Kasparov plays ... ♖xe2+ on the board. After a little confusion the demonstration board operators reveal the move to the crowd. This time it is the other co-Chief Arbiter, Bulgarian Andrei Malchev, who is left waving his arms in the air to plead for silence as the spectators break into appreciative applause.

Of the open sealed move Lincoln Lucena, a Brazilian chess official and journalist, said: "Two in a row – it could be the start of a new fashion". There was an unusual follow-up the next day at move 50 when the demonstrators put White's bishop on h7, misplaying the move. There was then a flurry of further moves, and reporters looked at each other nonplussed, not knowing what Karpov's 50th move had been. Confirmation eventually came half an hour later, but not before a witty Soviet journalist had described White's 50th as a "secret move". He seemed to be implying that since we were now entering the era of open sealed moves it was probably also time for a few secret open moves.

Dr Rafael Tudela, the Venezuelan Deputy President of FIDE, was also much in evidence during this game, having been left in charge during Campomanes's absence in Greece. Tudela commented to us: "Kasparov has grown in stature since the last match. There is no question that he is very much in control. His initial weaknesses of too much emotion and youth are gone. On the other hand, Karpov seems to be the victim of some kind of psychological disadvantage. I think the 5-0 score is flashing in his mind continuously."

Karpov-Kasparov
Queen's Gambit Declined

1	d4	0	d5	2
2	c4	0	e6	2
3	♘c3	0	♗e7	3
4	cd	0	ed	3
5	♗f4	0		

Maybe hoping for a sharp struggle after 5 ... c6 6 e3 ♗f5 7 g4!?.

5	...		♘f6	5
6	♕c2	10		

If 6 e3 ♗f5 7 ♕b3 ♘c6 8 ♕xb7 ♘b4 9 ♗b5+ ♔f8 and Black is better.

6	...		0-0	22
7	e3	15	c5	25
8	dc	23	♗xc5	30
9	♘f3	30	♘c6	31
10	♗e2	38	d4	34

Heading for almost total equality if he can overcome White's slight lead in development.

11	ed	43

If 11 0-0-0 ♕a5 12 ed ♗b4! with counterplay. Or 11 ... ♘b4 12 ♕b1 dc 13 ♖xd8 cb+ 14 ♔xb2 ♖xd8 with good compensation for the queen.

11	...		♘xd4	40
12	♘xd4	43	♕xd4	40
13	♗g3	43	♗e6	74
14	0-0	47	♖ac8	78
15	♗f3	52	b6	79
16	♖fe1	66	♕b4	89

Introducing a neat manoeuvre.

17	♗e5	94	♗d4	89

In *Sovietsky Sport* Gufeld gives 17 ... ♘d7 18 ♖e4 ♕a5 19 ♖a4 ♘xe5 20 ♖xa5 ♘xf3+ 21 gf ♗xa5 – another interesting queen sacrifice.

18	a3	96	♕c5	90
19	♗xd4	97	♕xd4	91
20	♖ad1	97	♕c5	95
21	♕a4	106	a5	97
22	♕d4	107	♕xd4	100
23	♖xd4	107	♖fd8	101
24	♖ed1	107	♖xd4	101
25	♖xd4	107	♔f8	102
26	♔f1	101	♔e7	105
27	♔e2	101	♗b3	115
28	♔e3	104	♖c5	120
29	♔d2	112	h6	122
30	♗e2	119	♘e8	133

If 30 ... ♘d5 31 ♗d1 ♘xc3 32 ♗xb3 ♘b5 33 ♖e4+ ±.

31	♗f3	124	♘f6	134
32	♖d3	128	♖e5	139
33	h3	129	♖c5	140
34	♖d4	129	♖c8	141
35	♗e2	130	♖c5	141
36	♗d3	131	h5	142
37	g3	133	g6	143
38	♘e2	135	♘d7	144
39	♖e4+	138	♖e5	145
40	♘d4	138	♗d5	145
41	♖e2	139	♖xe2+	151

110

The open sealed move.

42	**♗xe2**	*139*	**♘c5**	*152*
43	**♘b5**	*141*	**♘e4+**	*162*
44	**♔e3**	*142*	**♘d6**	*162*
45	**♔d4**	*146*	**♗c6**	*165*
46	**♘xd6**	*151*	**♔xd6**	*166*
47	**♗c4**	*152*	**♗e8**	*166*
48	**h4**	*152*	**f6**	*166*
49	**♗g8**	*180*	**♔c6**	*167*
50	**♗a2**	*181*	**♔d6**	*170*
51	**♗d5**	*181*	**♔e7**	*170*
52	**♗g8**	*185*	**♔d6**	*171*
53	**♗b3**	*185*	**♔e7**	*172*
54	**♗d1**	*186*	**♔d6**	*173*
55	**♗e2**	*189*	**♗d7**	*180*
56	**♗d3**	*190*	**♗e8**	*180*
57	**♗c4**	*190*	**♔e7**	*180*
58	**♗e2**	*190*	**♔d6**	*181*

White's advantage is mainly optical.

59	**g4**	*190*	**hg**	*183*
60	**♗xg4**	*190*	**♗f7**	*213*
61	**f4**	*194*	**f5**	*220*
62	**♗d1**	*195*	**♗d5**	*220*
63	**♗a4**	*195*	**♗f3**	*221*
64	**♗b3**	*197*	**♗e2**	*225*
65	**♗f7**	*202*	**♗h5**	*225*
66	**♔c4**	*202*	**♗e2+**	*227*
67	**♔c3**	*202*	**♗h5**	*228*
68	**b4**	*202*	**♔e7**	*231*
69	**♗c4**	*205*	**♔d6**	*232*
70	**ba**	*205*	**ba**	*232*
71	**♔d4**	*206*	**♗f3**	*233*
72	**♗f1**	*210*	**♗d5**	*236*
73	**♗e2**	*210*	**♗c6**	*237*
74	**♗d1**	*215*	**♗d5**	*241*
75	**♔e3**	*224*	**♔c5**	*243*
76	**♗a4**	*224*	**♗f7**	*243*
77	**♗d7**	*228*	**♔c4**	*253*
78	**a4**	*228*		

B

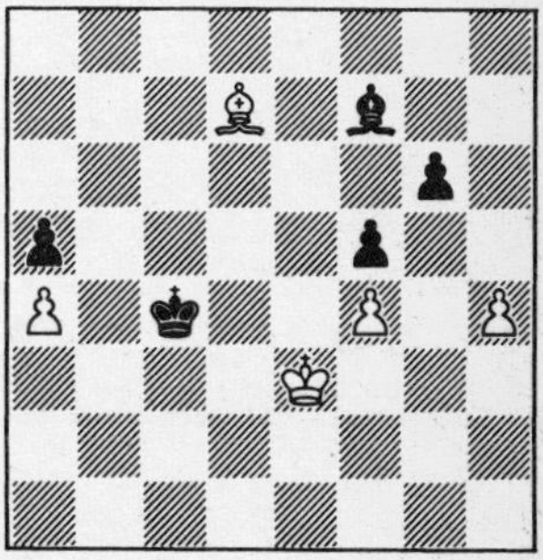

78	**...**		**♔c5!**	*254*

Black is alert at the critical moment. After 78 ... ♔c3 79 ♗b5! or 78 ... ♔b4 79 ♔d4 ♗b3 80 ♗e8 ♗xa4 81 ♗xg6 ♗b3! 82 ♗e8 Black holds but with more difficulty.

79	**♗b5**	*229*	**♔d5**	*262*
80	**♔d3**	*229*	**♔c5**	*262*
81	**♔c3**	*230*	**♔d6**	*263*
82	**♔d4**	*230*	**♗b3**	*263*
83	**♗e8**	*231*	**♔e7**	*266*
84	**♗xg6**	*233*	**♗xa4**	*266*
85	**♗xf5**	*233*	**♔f6**	*268*

Draw Agreed

Ironically, White has finally won a pawn, but it is useless for winning purposes.

Karpov	**0**	**½**	**½**	**1**	**1**	**½**	**½**	**½**	**½**	**½**	**0**	**½**	**½**	**½**	**½**	**0**	**½**	**½**	**0**	**½**	**9**
Kasparov	**1**	**½**	**½**	**0**	**0**	**½**	**½**	**½**	**½**	**½**	**1**	**½**	**½**	**½**	**½**	**1**	**½**	**½**	**1**	**½**	**11**

GAME TWENTY-ONE, 31 October-1 November

As the match enters its final stages, we witness a great surprise when Kasparov adjourns in what seems to be a very favourable ending. Chess lovers cancel their evening's plans expecting a long playing session, then suddenly Kasparov agrees a draw – particularly odd in view of his uncompromising play in the first session.

In an aggressive line of the Exchange Variation, Karpov produces an interesting new move. But Kasparov manages to gain the advantage after Karpov offers a faulty exchange of bishops. With the GM room crammed full and both players running short of time, the atmosphere is reminiscent of game 16 as onlookers strain on tiptoe to see what is being analysed. After Kasparov's 27th the position really begins to look good for White, and his advantage seems to increase in the time-scramble. Kasparov thinks for several minutes on his obvious 41st recapture, considering whether to seal (and, of course, if you're going to seal such an obvious move, you might as well reveal it) – teasing the expectant crowd. But it isn't going to be three in a row, and eventually he moves, leaving Karpov to stew over his sealed move on the stage. Taimanov says the adjourned position is very good for White, while Roman Toran (FIDE Deputy President for Europe) says pessimistically: "completely hopeless".

On the evening chess programme next day, Averbakh was asked why Kasparov had settled for an early draw in the second session. He agreed that White could have caused more problems and suggested, not without sarcasm, that for the best answer one should ask the players. The two concrete reasons he was able to suggest were that exchanges would increase drawing chances and that Kasparov preferred not to take risks.

112

Kasparov-Karpov
Queen's Gambit Declined

1	d4	0	d5	0			
2	c4	1	e6	0			
3	♘c3	3	♗e7	0			
4	cd	23	ed	0			
5	♗f4	23	c6	3			
6	e3	24	♗f5	6			
7	g4	24	♗e6	6			
8	h4!	25					

The most aggressive here. It is a move promulgated by Kasparov's mentor, Botvinnik, as an improvement on the 8 h3 which he personally introduced in his 1963 match versus Petrosian. 8 h3 also brought Korchnoi victory in game 13 v Karpov at Merano 1981.

8 ... ♘d7 17

A sample of what occurs if Black accepts the pawn sacrifice is 8 ... ♗xh4 9 ♕b3 g5 10 ♗h2 ♕b6! 11 ♘f3 ♕xb3 12 ab ♗xg4 13 ♘xh4 gh 14 ♗xb8 ♖xb8 15 ♖xa7 ± (analysis by Psakhis and Vaiser).

9 h5 26 ♘h6 17

An obviously prepared novelty, hoping to improve on 9 ... ♕b6 10 ♖b1 ♘f6 11 f3 0-0 12 ♗d3 c5 13 ♘ge2, Belyavsky-Geller, USSR Ch 1983.

10 ♗e2 36

10 ♗xh6 gh achieves nothing.

10 ... ♘b6 23

11 ♖c1 48 ♗d6?! 51

A mistake. It would have been far better to play 11 ... ♘c4 12 ♕b3

b5, or 12 b3 ♘d6.

12	♘h3	55	♗xf4	51	
13	♘xf4	55	♗d7	53	
14	♖g1	65	g5	71	

Maybe 14 ... ♕g5!? to blockade the black squares.

15	hg	75	hg	71	
16	♔d2	75	♕e7	75	
17	b3	85	g5	83	
18	♘d3	85	0-0-0	88	
19	♖h1	96	f6	89	
20	♕g1!	100			

Kasparov's strategy is original and interesting. He posts his king in the centre and infiltrates his queen into action via the extreme right flank.

20	...		♘f7	99	
21	♕g3	101	♕d6	102	
22	♕xd6	107	♘xd6	102	
23	f3	110			

White has two trumps: pressure on the h-file and the possibility of pressing forwards with his centre pawns.

23	...		♖dg8	111	
24	♘c5	118	♔d8	116	
25	♗d3	128	♗c8	117	

113

| 26 | ♘e2 | *130* | ♘a8 | *124* |
| 27 | ♗h7 | *132* | | |

This is reminiscent of Karpov-Unzicker, Nice Olympiad 1974, where Karpov played ♗a7 as White in a Ruy Lopez and then doubled rooks in the rear on the a-file. Karpov's bishop stayed on a7 for 20 moves, tying Black down, while Karpov organised a winning attack on the other wing.

27	...		♖f8	*128*
28	♖h6	*133*	♘c7	*128*
29	♘g3	*135*	♘f7	*134*
30	♖h2	*137*	♘e6	*134*
31	♘d3	*137*	♘g7	*134*
32	♖ch1	*139*	♔e7	*135*
33	♘f2	*140*	♖d8	*137*
34	♗f5	*145*	♖xh2	*145*
35	♖xh2	*147*	♘xf5	*145*
36	gf	*147*	♖h8	*146*
37	♖xh8	*147*	♘xh8	*146*
38	e4	*147*	♘f7	*147*
39	♘g4	*147*	♘d6	*148*
40	♘e3	*149*	de	*149*
41	fe	*152*	b6!!	*168*

The sealed move. It is the only chance, and perhaps one underestimated by all the Moscow experts. Passive defence against the threatened e5 is hopeless, e.g. 41 ... ♘f7 42 ♘g4 ♘d6 43 ♔e3 ♗d7 44 ♘h5 ♘e8 45 ♘h6 followed by e5 and if necessary ♘g8+.

| 42 | b4 | *153* | | |

A surprising move, after which Black activates his pieces. If White can win, it must be with 42 e5, but then 42 ... ♘b5 with the idea of ... c5 and ... ♗a6 could be annoying. Kasparov was evidently concerned that any advance of his pawns would weaken them and expose them to possible counterattack.

42	...		♗a6	*168*
43	♘g4	*155*	♘b5	*168*
44	♔d3	*176*	♘a3+	*170*

Draw Agreed

If 45 ♔e3 ♘c2+ or 45 ♔c3 ♘b5+.

| Karpov | 0 ½ ½ 1 1 ½ ½ ½ ½ ½ 0 ½ ½ ½ ½ 0 ½ ½ 0 ½ ½ | 9½ |
| Kasparov | 1 ½ ½ 0 0 ½ ½ ½ ½ ½ 1 ½ ½ ½ ½ 1 ½ ½ 1 ½ ½ | 11½ |

GAME TWENTY-TWO, 5 November

Karpov's victory in game 22 suddenly leaves the destination of the supreme chess title wide open again. With a one point lead and only two games left Kasparov, on paper, remains the favourite, but Karpov has nerves of steel, having acquired immense experience of tense conclusions from two of his past matches against Viktor Korchnoi.

Game 22 was a magnificent fighting achievement by Karpov, who struck down his young opponent in a classic game of manoeuvre. Kasparov's opening play was eccentric but in spite of this the situation appeared roughly balanced. But as the middlegame proceeded Kasparov fell into increasing time trouble, while Karpov gradually encroached with a systematic advance of his pawn majority on the king's wing.

Kasparov's decisive errors came with his impatient 31st and 35th moves. The net effect of these two blunders was to allow Karpov to transpose into a winning rook and pawn ending, which Kasparov resigned by telephone next morning. Far from making an open sealed move, it turned out to be particularly difficult to discover what Karpov's 42nd move had actually been. Even by the start of play in the next game there was still doubt as to whether he had played 42 ♖c7 or 42 ♔g4.

Karpov-Kasparov
Queen's Gambit Declined

1	d4	*0*	d5	*1*
2	c4	*0*	e6	*2*
3	♘c3	*0*	♗e7	*3*
4	cd	*0*	ed	*3*
5	♗f4	*0*	♘f6	*3*

Kasparov avoids Karpov's own choice, 5 ... c6.

6	e3	*0*	0-0	*4*
7	♘f3	*4*	♗f5!?	*6*

A provocative move. More in Kasparov's style is 7 ... c5, but in this crucial game he probably wanted to avoid an isolated queen's pawn.

8	h3!?	*25*

Displaying a resolute frame of mind. After 8 ♕b3 ♘c6 9 ♕xb7 ♘b4 Black enjoys dangerous counterplay.

8	...	**c6**	37
9	**g4**	32	

Continuing in the same courageous vein. With his back to the wall Karpov displays great courage. The text is very aggressive, but also implies a loosening of his own position.

9	...	**♗g6**	55

9 ... ♗e4 is worth a thought.

10	**♘e5**	32	**♘fd7**	57
11	**♘xg6**	36	**fg!?**	57

A remarkable decision which weakens the e6 square and cedes White a potential future majority of pawns in the centre or on the king's flank. After 11 ... hg perhaps Black feared that White might follow up with ♗d3, ♕c2 and 0-0-0, later attacking on the king's wing with h4. By opening the f-file, Kasparov makes this procedure more difficult.

12	**♗g2**	40	**♘b6**	61
13	**0-0**	44	**♔h8**	78
14	**♘e2**	51	**g5**	82

Not a pleasant move to make, but he has to prevent ♘f4.

15	**♗g3**	52	**♗d6**	83

Ensuring that White will not retain the bishop pair. After the exchange White cannot activate his pawn majority by means of f3 plus e4 since this would leave a horrible weakness on f4.

16	**♕d3**	57	**♘a6**	87
17	**b3**	65		

Hemming in Black's knights.

17	...	**♕e7**	91
18	**♗xd6**	73	**♕xd6**	91
19	**f4!**	73		

In order to make progress White has no choice but to concede a weak square on e3. The compensation is his mobile mass of kingside pawns which can crowd Black's pieces and which may eventually produce a passed pawn.

19	...	**gf**	106
20	**ef**	73	**♖ae8**	108
21	**f5**	82	**♘c7**	110
22	**♖f2**	87	**♘d7**	114
23	**g5**	90	**♕e7**	119
24	**h4**	98		

It looks tempting to play 24 ♕g3 ♘b5 25 ♕h4, though this allows invasion of his own lines with ... ♕e3. Karpov prefers to proceed methodically, not shunning the exchange of queens.

24	...	**♕e3**	122
25	**♖d1**	98	**♘b5**	124

116

26	♕xe3	105	♖xe3	124
27	♔h2	105	♘b6	130
28	♘g3	111	♘c8	132
29	♘f1	118		

Repelling boarders – the point of this and White's next.

29	...		♖e7	133
30	♖d3	120	♘cd6	134
31	♘g3	121		

| 31 | ... | | ♘e4? | 137 |

Much too hasty. He should re-invade with 31 ... ♖e1!, when the position is not clear. White's asset, the kingside pawns, can also turn out to be a weakness. Some Moscow commentators (Kasparov fans?) even preferred Black's chances after the correct move.

32	♗xe4	122	de	137
33	♖e3	122	♘xd4	140
34	♔h3!	132		

Typically Karpovian. Of course he cannot capture on e4, but the direct 34 f6 gf 35 gf.♖e6 36 ♖xe4 is enticing. The text screws up the tension to unbearable levels, and in time trouble Kasparov cracks.

| 34 | ... | | ♖e5 | 146 |
| 35 | ♔g4 | 135 | h5+?? | 148 |

Anything but this impetuous shot.

36	♔xh5	136	♘xf5	148
37	♖xf5	136	♖8xf5	148
38	♘xf5	136	♖xf5	148
39	♖xe4	136	♔h7	148

If 39 ... ♔g8 40 ♔g6 ♖f7 41 ♖e8+ ♖f8 42 ♖e7 wins.

| 40 | ♖e7 | 137 | b5 | 148 |

Or 40 ... ♖b5 41 a4! ♖xb3 42 g6+.

| 41 | ♖xa7 | 138 | b4 | 152 |

A typical win now would be 42 ♖c7 and if 42 ... c5 then 43 ♔g4 ♖d5 44 h5 (threatening h6) 44 ... ♔g8 45 g6 ♔f8 46 ♖c8+ ♔e7 47 h6 queening a pawn.

Karpov actually sealed

| 42 | ♔g4 | 153 | | |

which makes little difference, and **Kasparov resigned** without resuming.

| Karpov | 0 | ½ | ½ | 1 | 1 | ½ | ½ | ½ | ½ | ½ | 0 | ½ | ½ | ½ | ½ | 0 | ½ | ½ | 0 | ½ | ½ | 1 | 10½ |
| Kasparov | 1 | ½ | ½ | 0 | 0 | ½ | ½ | ½ | ½ | ½ | 1 | ½ | ½ | ½ | ½ | 1 | ½ | ½ | 1 | ½ | ½ | 0 | 11½ |

GAME TWENTY-THREE, 7 November

Moscow is awash with red flags, slogans and giant portraits of Lenin as the November 7th celebrations get underway. As Soviets throughout the land honour their national day, a crowd began to form outside the Tchaikovsky Hall. Kasparov's car arrives first, but it is the Champion who receives the greater ovation in the street. Inside the Hall the situation is reversed as the Challenger receives a loud and lengthy ovation from the appreciative spectators, while applause for Karpov is polite and short.

As the illuminations began to go on throughout Moscow, Kasparov flashed out his opening, while Karpov moved more slowly and circumspectly. Playing solely to avoid any risk of losing, Kasparov built up a small and quiet advantage from the opening. Although it was the kind of position which Karpov is famous for defending well, he could not afford to adjourn with more than small losing chances. By move 30 there was universal expectation that the game would be adjourned. While some stressed the arduous nature of Black's defensive task, others such as Suetin felt that Karpov might have adequate defensive resources. When Karpov survived his time trouble and the two players agreed a draw, everybody applauded, partly for the fine game but also as a mark of respect for Karpov's defensive dexterity.

It is ironic that after 71 games and eight months of title matches, the title itself still hangs solely on Saturday's final game.

Kasparov-Karpov
Queen's Gambit Declined

1	d4	0	d5	0
2	c4	0	e6	0
3	♘c3	1	♗e7	0
4	♘f3	4	♘f6	0
5	♗g5	4	h6	3
6	♗xf6	5	♗xf6	7
7	e3	5	0-0	10

8 Rc1   7

Quieter than 8 Wd2 or 8 Wc2, indicating that Kasparov wants to play for a slight edge with no risks at all.

8	...		c6	18
9	Bd3	8	Nd7	24
10	0-0	9	dc	33
11	Bxc4	10	e5	33
12	h3	11	ed	46
13	ed	12	Nb6	48
14	Bb3	12	Re8	68
15	Re1	13	Bf5	75
16	Rxe8+	15	Wxe8	75
17	Wd2	15		

White has his small edge. The bishop on b3 is difficult to neutralise.

17	...		Wd7	85
18	Re1	16	Rd8	99
19	Wf4	20	Nd5	108
20	Nxd5	25	cd	108
21	Ne5	25		

Karpov's choice now leaves him with a permanent inferiority. 21

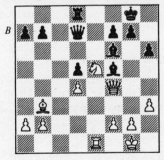

... We6 would be more risky but more ambitious, e.g. 22 Nd3 Bg5! or 22 h4 Bh7 and then ... Wf5.

21	...		Bxe5	116
22	Rxe5	30	Be6	116
23	We3	64	Kf8	116
24	Wd3	74		

Black was threatening ... Re8 and ... f6.

24	...		f6	122
25	Re1	80	Bf7	126
26	Wc3	84	Wd6	128
27	Rc1	87	Be8	130
28	Bd1	99	a6	138
29	Bf3	102	g6	140
30	h4	113	h5	141
31	g3	118	Bf7	144
32	a4	124	Rd7	145
33	a5	126	Kg7	145
34	Wb3	130	We6	146
35	Wb4	132	We8	147
36	Kg2	135	Wd8	148
37	Rc5?			

Perhaps 37 Re1, to meet ... g5 in the future with hg and then Re5. Another promising idea is 37 Wc3 to be followed by Kh2, Bg2 and Bh3. After the text Karpov activates efficiently and White's advantage melts away.

37	...		We7	
38	Wc3		g5	
39	We3		g4	
40	Bd1		We4+	
41	Kg1		Draw Agreed	

Karpov   0 ½ ½ 1 1 ½ ½ ½ ½ ½ 0 ½ ½ ½ ½ 0 ½ ½ 0 ½ ½ 1 ½ 11

Kasparov 1 ½ ½ 0 0 ½ ½ ½ ½ ½ 1 ½ ½ ½ ½ 1 ½ ½ 1 ½ ½ 0 ½ 12

GAME TWENTY-FOUR, 9 November

Kasparov takes the final game, thus becoming, at age 22, the thirteenth World Champion and the youngest in the century-long history of the championship. Karpov as White launches a vigorous attack against Black's king but then he is stopped dead in his tracks by an ingenious pawn sacrifice. At first observers are very confused and Dorfman anxiously comments: "Maybe Gary has enough compensation, but it seems dangerous given the match score". But Kasparov has it all worked out, and as Karpov's clock ticks away the grandmasters decide that Black's chances are certainly sufficient for a draw.

But Karpov cannot acquiesce in sharing the point. In striving for more he stumbles into a further sacrifice followed by a blitz counter-offensive and finally the laying waste of the entire White position during the Champion's desperate time trouble. When Karpov concedes the title he has held for ten years, pandemonium breaks out in the Hall, with frenetic fans chanting and cheering. Protests from frustrated officials that "this is chess – not football", go unheeded.

The game has been worthy of the great occasion. It was conducted with immense courage and resource by both players. David Bronstein remarked: "It's probably one of the greatest games Kasparov has ever played. His final attack was absolutely brilliant, and I hope he can continue to produce such stunning chess for us in the future". As the crowds cheered and stamped, Lincoln Lucena said: "Young people all over the world were waiting for this moment. It was a very important result."

At the moment of victory, when Karpov extended his hand, Kasparov turned towards the audience and, savouring the moment, raised his arms high. This dramatic moment was captured in a freeze-frame on that evening's TV analysis programme.

After Kasparov left the stage the din increased, with spectators stomping, clapping and chanting. As Kasparov was departing from the Hall, some of those waiting outside cried out: "Zaftra, zaftra" ("tomorrow"). But suddenly the news filtered through from the Hall that Kasparov had already won, and soon the familiar cries of "Gary, Gary" were ringing out again.

As he was getting into his curtained black Volga, AP reporter Alison Smale asked Kasparov how he felt. A beaming Kasparov raised up his arms and said: "Otlichno" ("excellent"). Then, with his seconds in the back congratulating and hugging each other, the Kasparovmobile swept away down Gorky Street accompanied by its habitual police escort. These jubilant scenes were in stark contrast to the earlier nerves and tension. A quarter of an hour later, Karpov emerged, but understandably he refused to comment.

Karpov-Kasparov
Sicilian Najdorf/Scheveningen

1	e4	*0*			

We find it somewhat strange that Karpov should resort to the king's pawn for this death-or-glory game. He has not beaten Kasparov with 1 e4 since game 3 of their first match. His results with 1 d4 have been much superior.

1	...		c5	*0*	
2	♘f3	*0*	d6	*1*	
3	d4	*0*	cd	*1*	
4	♘xd4	*1*	♘f6	*1*	
5	♘c3	*2*	a6	*1*	
6	♗e2	*2*	e6	*2*	
7	0-0	*3*	♗e7	*2*	
8	f4	*3*	0-0	*3*	
9	♔h1	*3*	♕c7	*3*	
10	a4	*4*	♘c6	*3*	
11	♗e3	*4*	♖e8	*3*	
12	♗f3	*5*	♖b8	*4*	
13	♕d2	*7*	♗d7	*6*	
14	♘b3	*8*	b6	*6*	
15	g4!?	*8*			

The first new move and the only time in this match that Karpov has launched a direct attack against the king. This thrust is highly aggressive but also loosening.

15	...		♗c8	*13*	
16	g5	*8*	♘d7	*14*	
17	♕f2	*9*	♗f8	*31*	
18	♗g2	*10*	♗b7	*31*	
19	♖ad1	*19*	g6	*34*	
20	♗c1	*63*	♖bc8	*60*	
21	♖d3	*70*	♘b4	*71*	
22	♖h3!?	*70*			

The natural follow-up to his previous retreat with the queen's bishop, but the attack introduced with this move evinces a bucolic flavour. White can hardly hope to blast through with ♕h4, and it is more likely that his plan was to

121

steer for f5, in combination, perhaps, with ♗e3-d4.

| 22 | ... | | ♗g7 | 73 |
| 23 | ♗e3 | 73 | ♖e7! | 101 |

A profound prophylactic manoeuvre. Black's rook defends f7
directly, h7 distantly and prepares
to meet 24 ♗d4 with 24 ... e5 25 fe
de. There is also a further deeper
point, as we shall see.

| 24 | ♔g1 | 102 | ♖ce8! | 116 |

An amazing intensification of
Black's prophylactic strategy. Nimzowitsch used to describe the action
of placing one rook on a closed file
as "mysterious", but this is doubly
so, and all the more astounding
given the confined space in which
the rooks can operate. One of
Black's ideas is to meet 25 f5 with
25 ... ef, when his rooks will storm
down the e-file. A second idea is to
play ... f5 himself, even as a pawn
sacrifice.

25	♖d1	103	f5	125
26	gf	105	♘xf6	125
27	♖g3	113		

Stopping ... ♘g4. If 27 ♗xb6 at
once, either 27 ... ♕b8, as in the
game, or even 27 ... ♘g4 with huge
complications.

27	...		♖f7	130
28	♗xb6	114	♕b8	130
29	♗e3	122	♘h5	132
30	♖g4	127		

If 30 ♖f3 then Black also plays
30 ... ♘f6.

| 30 | ... | | ♘f6 | 135 |
| 31 | ♖h4? | 132 | | |

Objectively, White must play 31
♖g3, inviting a draw by repetition,
but that would be equivalent to
abdication of his title.

| 31 | ... | | g5!! | 138 |

A fantastically strong move
which frees the shackles from
Black's entire army.

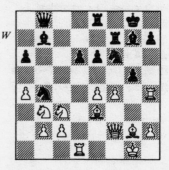

32	fg	132	♘g4	138
33	♕d2	145	♘xe3	138
34	♕xe3	146	♘xc2	139
35	♕b6	146		

Any other sensible queen move
would allow 35 ... ♕a7+.

| 35 | ... | | ♗a8 | 142 |

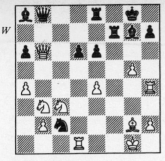

36 Rxd6? *147*

In appalling time trouble Karpov sheds a piece, but 36 Qxb8 Rxb8 is also highly unpleasant given Black's b-file pressure and raking bishops, and the scattered nature of White's own forces.

36	...		Rb7	*143*
37	**Qxa6**	*147*	Rxb3	*143*
38	**Rxe6**	*147*	Rxb2	*144*
39	**Qc4**	*149*	Kh8	*147*
40	**e5??**	*149*		

A blunder, but the position is already lost.

40	...		Qa7+	*148*
41	**Kh1**	*149*	Bxg2+	*150*

42	**Kxg2**	*149*	Nd4+	*151*

Even more accurate than 42 ... Ne3+. Of course, Black does not fall for 42 ... Rxe6?? 43 Qc8+, when White would have retained his title.

White resigns

An historic final position for one of the most important games of chess ever played. At its close Kasparov paid generous tribute to his defeated opponent: "I should like to point out that Anatoly Karpov put up a grand fight. I felt it morally and physically . . . He played very strongly in this match."

Kasparov	1	½	½	0	0	½	½	½	½	½	1	½	½	½	½	1	½	½	1	½	½	0	½	1	13
Karpov	0	½	½	1	1	½	½	½	½	½	0	½	½	½	½	0	½	½	0	½	½	1	½	0	11

CONCLUSION

After game 15 of last year's super-K match (with the win tally 4-0 in his favour) Karpov surprisingly mentioned that he now expected a long series of draws. Superstition or premonition? Since then Anatoly and Gary have contested no fewer than 47 drawn games, and in the process the name of the Champion has changed from Karpov to Kasparov.

Following Karpov's fine start, what caused this deadlock in their previous match? Karpov's colossal initial lead may have deluded him into believing that he could simply rely on a Kasparov blunder to win. How wrong he was! Kasparov dug in his heels and wrestled the Champion to a standstill. In this lengthy process Kasparov dared not display his full powers of imagination in case of an accidental loss, but he did acquire from Karpov involuntary instruction in the art of consolidation.

In this fresh match, with the initial score of 0-0, both sides were able to display their true talents to the fullest extent. Karpov revealed the positional and strategic mastery of his hero Capablanca, especially in the simplified situations of games 4 and 22. Meanwhile, Kasparov fused the deep openings research of his tutor, Botvinnik, with the dynamism of Alekhine and (a new element) the restless imagination and depth of Nimzowitsch. The games were of a universally high quality, and in our opinion Kasparov's achievement excels even that of Bobby Fischer against Spassky in 1972. Karpov's resistance was certainly much more impressive than Spassky's, even though he may have been handicapped by nervousness concerning the *Spiegel* allegations published at the mid-point of the match.

Perhaps Kasparov will now feel slightly less bitter about the closure of the first match. But having lost his title it is perhaps Karpov who will feel himself the injured party by Campomanes' intervention last February. Apropos the FIDE President, had one of his requests been carried out, this book could not have been written in its present form. Campomanes sent a pre-match telex to the USSR Chess Federation urging that co-author David Goodman and Gary's friend Eric Schiller should not be granted visas. To their great credit the Soviet Federation refused to kowtow and duly issued a visa to David.

As Kasparov said at the final conference, "The creative dispute between Karpov and myself is not over". Within three days of Kasparov's coronation as Champion, FIDE had invited bids for the revenge match, starting as soon as 10 February 1986. There are some who question the notion of an almost immediate rematch after the 72 games they have already played. Speeding through autumnal Moscow in his black Volga, Kasparov told Jon Tisdall, Dominic Lawson and the authors that if a rematch were to take place he would be willing to play it in London.

London played a great role in Kasparov's path to the world title by rescuing and restaging his forfeited semi-final against Korchnoi. Thanks to the Greater London Council and Tim Rice's *CHESS* musical, the capital now has the resources to bid for this revenge match.

Kasparov is now quickly rebuilding his bridges with the Soviet chess establishment, but is continuing to criticize FIDE President Campomanes. Over a dinner of caviar and crab at his Moscow camp, Kasparov spoke with co-author Goodman and Jon Tisdall in his first interview with Western reporters as Champion. Commenting on Campomanes he said: "One man cannot solve all the problems in chess", and referring to his own role he stated: "I am the chess king, but I would like to see democracy in chess". In the final minutes he spoke of his hopes for the future. "Chess is good for connections between peoples and countries, and as a chess-player and sportsman I am waiting for the new détente. Détente is the best situation for connections between sport and culture."